TODAY'S INSPIRED LATINA

Volume II

LIFE STORIES OF SUCCESS IN THE FACE OF ADVERSITY

JACKIE CAMACHO-RUIZ

Today's Inspired Latina

This book is a compilation of stories from numerous Latinas who have each contributed a chapter and is designed to provide inspiration to our readers.

It is sold with the understanding that the publisher and the individual authors are not engaged in the rendering of psychological, legal, accounting or other professional advice. The content and views in each chapter are the sole expression and opinion of its author and not necessarily the views of Fig Factor Media, LLC.

For more information, contact:

Jaqueline Camacho-Ruiz
Fig Factor Media, LLC | JJR Marketing, Inc. (parent company)
jackie@jjrmarketing.com | www.jjrmarketing.com

Cover Design & Layout by Juan Pablo Ruiz
Printed in the United States of America

ISBN: 978-0-9971605-0-5

To all the future Latina leaders
who believe in something greater than
themselves. This book is for you.

Contents:

Acknowledgements

Today's Inspired Latina Vol I authors: without you, this dream would not be a reality. Thank you from the bottom of my heart for believing in me and the magic that our first book has created in our lives.

I would like to express my special thanks to all the team members that made this book happen. Juan Pablo, the love of my life and business partner for your relentless support and vision on this project. Karen Dix for your dedication and love to every story. A very special thanks to Irene Anzola for your incredible passion, positive attitude and due diligence in working with every single author as the project manager.

To all of you that have believed in coming together to make an impact.

Introduction

JACQUELINE CAMACHO-RUIZ

They say seeing is believing, and I think that's true. When the world got a look at the first volume of "Today's Inspired Latina," everyone began to believe!

These brave authors, who believed in themselves enough to share their stories with the world, found others believed in them too. Their lives changed almost immediately as many of them launched businesses, podcasts and television and radio shows. Some shared their motivational stories as paid speakers for the first time ever. More than 30 local and national media outlets including INC. Magazine and WGN pursued the Volume 1 authors for more of their words of wisdom. The biggest achievement, however, was that the words of these giving ladies touched the hearts of countless Latinas, including the next generation, who are so hungry for comfort, inspiration and empowerment.

Volume I authors were all from Chicago and invited to be part of this effort. I'm proud to say that this volume grew organically, from word of mouth and ladies across the country requesting to be part of it. At our national book tour through Chicago, New York City and Miami, Latinas took me aside and excitedly asked, "How do I get in the next one?" My heart soars with the thought of the journey these Latinas are about to take, and I won't be surprised that this movement may go international!

(Ladies from Mexico have already inquired about Volume 3!)

Perhaps the book speaks to people because it is a niche project for Latinas, and the stories are so inspiring. However, I believe the book also came along at just the right time. Latinas are ripe to become agents of change as they acculturate and embrace their potential. Through this project, I've learned that the power and influence of the Hispanic community is greater than I even realized, and is truly changing the face of America. And because of that, I think "Today's Inspired Latina" is a book that is fanning the flames of this nationwide movement!

Yes, seeing is believing. But the stories in "Today's Inspired Latina" are just the beginning. The power and pride that comes from Latina authorship will help this burgeoning movement not only be believed, but exalted!

Jacqueline Camacho-Ruiz

Today's Inpired Latina Founder. Author of The Little Book of Business Secrets that Work, The Fig Factor, The Fig Factor Journal, 200 Consejos Poderosos para Alcanzar el Éxito en los Negocios, Overcoming Mediocrity contributing author, and The Crusaders comic book superhero character.

Preface

NELI VAZQUEZ ROWLAND

President and Founder, A Safe Haven

For several years, mutual friends of Jackie and I kept telling us that we needed to meet. When we finally did, there was an instant connection between the two of us. We exchanged stories, we laughed, we cried, and we knew right away that we are true kindred spirits.

At that time, Jackie told me about a special project she was wrapping up called "Today's Inspired Latina". This project, her first book, would reveal the lives of many amazing and inspiring Latina women who, against all odds, overcame major obstacles while pursuing and achieving their dreams.

Personally, I am in the business of helping the homeless- our society's most challenged individuals- to rebuild their lives in a sustainable manner. Through this experience I have come to understand how environmental, physical, social, economic, and cultural challenges are often embedded in societal systems. In turn, without someone to believe in you and guide you through them, the result may be nothing short of hopelessness and despair.

Jackie instinctively understands what it feels like to face seemingly insurmountable circumstances. Yet, she confronts difficulties like she does all things in life: with a boundless, contagious, enthusiasm and optimism. Having overcome her own challenges, she draws on personal experience and compassion to give a voice to others who have also endured and successfully navigated life's rocky storms. This involves a gift of self; something that Jackie understands as her purpose and embodies in her actions. Her dedication to the Fig Factor Foundation, an organization doing so much good for young Latinas across our nation, is a true testament to her selflessness.

Traditionally, the Latino immigrant community is blessed with a long history of inspirational women. These women are not afraid to lead the way or work behind the scenes. Whatever the circumstances call for, they make the personal sacrifices needed to carve a path for all of us hoping to turn our dreams into reality.

Both Jackie's life and these stories illustrate the uniquely invigorating outcome of surrounding yourself with people who share your family and community values. By creating a deep connection between self and others, overwhelming challenges suddenly don't appear so difficult anymore.

I AM A PHOENIX

Mayra Rubio

"Don't wait until you die to be reborn. Your past does not define who you are, it's only muscle that you are building for your future."

"Kill me!" There I was, lying in the middle of 22nd Street on Apr. 27, 2009 at about 1 a.m. My husband of six years was hovering over my body, beating me. I laid on the concrete with my arms wide open. I had a clear shot at his groin, but I didn't fight back. Something told me not to move. I just watched him with an internal smile because I knew we were finally over. I didn't feel any pain, only him beating the pain of the past out of me and believe me, it felt great.

It was an out of body experience, like the scene in "Ghost" when Patrick Swayze is shot and his soul leaves his body and he sees himself lying there, lifeless. I watched everything as if it were happening in slow motion. And then I saw the light. He immediately snapped out of his trance, ran back around to his SUV and I got up. A car was coming.

He got in the driver seat and I stood outside the passenger door. My vision was blurred and I felt dizzy. I was trying to feel for my purse inside the truck because I couldn't see. "Let me get my purse," I said. He put the car in gear to drive while I was still searching with half my body in the car. The lights were coming closer. He was panicking because he thought it was a cop coming. I felt a coffee thermos in his cup holder. I grabbed it and cracked it on the side of his forehead before he sped off.

Without my cell phone or money, the single car heading straight towards me was my only hope. I flagged it down and it stopped. That's when all of my emotions came pouring out. "My husband just beat me, I need…." I heard a soft voice, "It's ok, calm down, get inside the car." The driver was a young girl going home from the gym who just happened to be the police dispatcher for Berkeley, the town where I lived. What were the chances? She immediately called an ambulance. I will never forget her and be forever grateful for that young girl who was brave enough to help a half-beaten stranger in the middle of the street. She was an angel sent from above.

That day was the day the naïve, weak me died. That day I vowed to never let another man lay a hand on me. The girl that constantly suffered, cried, fed, clothed and supported a man that didn't love or appreciate her in return didn't exist anymore.

The light that I had seen from the distance wasn't the car; it was the door that God opened for me. "This way out" was what I heard, and I never looked back.

STORMS OF LIFE

I am the youngest of four. My parents have been married for nearly 50 years, and my mom was about 40 when she had me. By then, my siblings were all almost teenagers, so growing up, I felt like I was the only child. But even though I am the youngest, I am the oldest soul of the family and have always been far more mature than my years. I was always a high honor student that lacked guidance.

By the tender age of 16, I became pregnant and by 17, I was a single mom. When my boyfriend abandoned me when I was eight months pregnant, I actually felt like I got away with my baby, free and clear.

My pregnancy was a blow for my parents. They raised great kids who were not involved with gangs or drugs, did well in school and behaved. When I got pregnant, they just didn't know how to handle it.

But I have always been very headstrong and so I embraced my pregnancy. I didn't care what others thought and my baby became my only care in the world. Nobody was going to rob me of the bond that I was experiencing with my child. Abortion was my parent's first brilliant idea, but if there is one thing that I am against in this world it's abortion. It was never an option for me.

My mom used to give a look that made me hear all the words she was saying inside about me. It didn't matter because I knew that everything was going to be all right. I knew my parents, though heartbroken, would never throw me out on the street.

When I was 19, I married by choice and by the age of 26, I was going through a divorce. Divorce is one of the most awful things that a human can endure, but I did it and I did it alone, without burdening my family. Two and a half years after my demise, I was free.

The years surrounding my divorce were the darkest, most difficult years of my life. My whole world came crashing down all at once. In October of 2008, I was trying to transition out of the mortgage industry and had just finished three long months of studying for my Series 7 stockbroker's license. I passed my exam and then the economy took a turn for the worse. I lost my job and a few short months after that I was applying for a restraining order from my husband, filing for divorce, and putting the house that I purchased when I was 19 years old on the market, only to run out of time after two different buyers backed out. I lost it in foreclosure after putting so much love into remodeling it.

I was under what felt like a permanent dark cloud. My only friend and greatest supporter at the time was another loan officer named Carlos, who I had met through my ex-husband. In April of 2009, right before my incident, Carlos had gotten me a job at a small mortgage broker shop.

After the incident, I took a week off because I didn't want anyone to see my wounds. When I told Carlos what happened to me, he told me that I could be the greatest loan officer in the world. He told me that I could be an inspiration to many women out there. Even though I felt like my life was at rock bottom, something inside of me felt that it was true. I just didn't understand how he was able to see that potential in me when I was half dead inside.

He kept me on my toes. He gave me inspirational books to

read. He made me laugh so hard my stomach would be sore for days. And that's how I got through until November.

BIRTH OF THE PHOENIX

Nov. 7, 2009 was the first weekend I did not have my kids because that's when visitation rights kicked in. I was going to meet some new friends at a lounge downtown and then end the night with Carlos. The whole night was filled with unfortunate events, and when I got to the club to meet Carlos, I couldn't find a parking space. I texted to ask him where I should park but he didn't answer right away like usual. I stood outside the car with no one in sight, looked up in the sky and I said to myself, "Mayra, you have no business being here, GO HOME!"

Sometimes we tell ourselves things and we don't listen. That night I did listen. By the time Carlos responded, I had gotten on the highway so I told him I was going home and to be safe. The next morning, a text message woke me up. It was from one of Carlos' friends. "Did you hear what happened to Carlos?" he said. "He's dead."

For a second I thought it was a hoax or a sick joke, but it was real. I had never experienced such a brutal loss. I spent my 27th birthday at my best friend's wake.

It took me several years to feel alive again. I felt like I should've been the one to die that night because I wasn't appreciating life. The hardest part of my day was getting up in the morning and at times I didn't even succeed. People would just look at me like a piece of fruit that was rotting away right before their eyes. No doctor, priest, psychic, or hypnotist could lift me from what seemed like eternal darkness.

I was my only hope. I was half dead but the higher power inside of me was very much alive. I realized this suffering of mine was a product of the thoughts in my head, the self that I had lost through my toxic marriage and the loss of a great friend. This darkness was a true blessing in disguise.

A phoenix is a mythical bird that is cyclically reborn. After a long life, the bird dies in a combustion of its own flames and a new, fully-grown phoenix emerges from the ashes. That is who I am.

I had to burn and let go of the past to envision the life I wanted for myself and my kids. I had to go back to the basics and visualize the career I wanted. I knew that whatever path I chose, I was going to make a difference for a few or many.

In 2013, I reconnected with a couple of friends and former colleagues of mine that had opened their own mortgage company a few years earlier. They had survived the recession and now operated one of the fastest growing mortgage companies in America. My initial meeting with them was to tell them I was getting out of the business. "You're not in the wrong business, you're with the wrong company," said my current boss. Those simple words had such an impact on me, even to this day. They not only apply to work but life alike and the people you share it with.

My new bosses took me in, whipped me into shape and brought me back to life! I have now helped hundreds of families (and counting!) change their lives by realizing their dreams of home ownership. I have a reborn passion for originating loans. I am a great producer and do very well for myself and my amazing and beautiful daughters. I am grateful to have bosses who are my biggest supporters and mentors and who see in me what Carlos did. They are my family.

The day to inspire has finally come. This is my biggest leap and I have so much more to accomplish. This is only a chapter in my life, not the whole book. Don't allow a chapter in your life to define who you are or where you are going. I have learned to steer clear of negative and envious people. People who immediately hate you are dealing with their own inner reflection. When you are positive, negative people don't have a place in your life.

Don't ever give up on yourself. Everything is temporary, good and bad. Embrace the journey and the rebirth that is awaiting you. Others may never give you another chance but you must give yourself another chance. God didn't slack on the making of us. We are all powerful creatures and our bodies regenerate themselves. When we get a paper cut, we heal. We are the master creators of our lives. Just ask with faith and conviction and the universe will provide.

Whatever your past or present story, embrace it, build your muscle, and go get the life that you desire. It's waiting for you!

REFLECTION

1. Do I want to spend the rest of my life as I am now?

2. What do I envision my life to include?

3. Do I have faith in myself to transform my life?

BIOGRAPHY

Mayra is a Senior Mortgage Banker at Neighborhood Loans. She has more than a decade of experience in the industry, and enjoys helping families realize their dream of home ownership. Neighborhood Loans has recognized her as a top producer. She works hand in hand with realtors to establish solid business relationships in the industry. Her hard work over the years has helped her become a preferred lender for builders, real estate brokerages, and investors.

Mayra attributes her success to her own persistence and the presence of wise mentors in her life who have given her opportunities. She truly believes everything happens for a reason and if you surround yourself with successful people, you will be a success. Mayra has a background in finance and real estate. She is a single mom, raising her daughters, Gisselle (16) and Serena (13) in Chicago. When not at work or spending time with her daughters, Mayra enjoys cooking, yoga, writing, crossfit and most of all, giving advice and motivating others when they need a little inspiration.

Mayra O. Rubio
mayra@neighborhoodloans.com
(708) 699-9776

LEARNING TO BE CONFIDENT

Angelica Monroy

"Embrace your vulnerabilities, accept them, and forgive yourself."

Have you ever wondered if every baby is born self-confident? I have, and I think they are.

Now, how do we help them remain confident throughout their childhood and early adult life?

When I think back to my early years, I remember feeling I could conquer the world. I climbed trees, wandered through the woods, talked to anyone that would listen to me, and made friends easily. I was a happy, fearless, and confident kid. Unfortunately, that feeling dissipated at some point. It is hard to tell where it went, when it left or what specifically took it away. The journey to regain it has been a long one. Although there were some unfortunate events during my childhood, the effects of such events became apparent during my adolescent years.

CONFIDENCE LOST AND FOUND

One of those changes came a day before my fifteenth birthday when my parents made the U.S. our permanent residence. When I first learned we were moving, I imagined America as a magical place. I pictured beautiful homes with grand landscapes and warm spacious rooms. I saw ample streets surrounded with flourishing green trees and an abundance of colorful flowers. A little part of me was nervous to leave everything I knew as home, but the excitement to be part of the beautiful, magical place I had created was much more inviting.

Then we arrived in the "windy city" (Chicago). It was August, so the temperature was comfortable, the trees were full of green leaves, and some areas of the city had beautiful gardens. Soon after, the leaves changed color and disappeared completely. The "windy city" became a true windy place, simply a new place to live. It didn't feel like home. In my mind, this was just a temporary place to live. I longed for the warm weather, the sunny days, the salty ocean waves, my friends, and the much cherished freedom I grew up with. The area of Chicago we moved to could not compare to the small, welcoming town I used to call home. "Home" was twenty minutes away from the beautiful beaches of Manzanillo. I walked everywhere in my little town: school, church, the recreational center, and friends' homes.

I arrived just in time to enter ninth grade, the interesting world of high school. My English vocabulary consisted of no more than ten words, yet I was enrolled in an English-only, all-girl, Catholic school. Due to my good grades, the school decided to give me an opportunity to prove my worth and not hold me back a grade.

Reading and writing was not an easy task for me so I took a strong liking to math. All I had to do was follow the sequence of numbers to get the correct answers. Math became therapeutic since it was a subject I excelled in, regardless of the limited English I spoke or understood.

I was determined to do well in school. I've always had a love for learning, so I decided to take English classes in the evening at a local community center. I also became friends with my neighbor next door, who spent several hours helping me with my homework during my first year of high school. I also made another good friend, the English-Spanish dictionary. I carried it around and referenced it all day long. After one year, I felt comfortable enough with the written part of the new language, completed my assignments with little or no help, and started enjoying the rest of my academic courses.

Academically, I was excelling. Socially, not so much. I went from confidently standing in front of a crowd and reciting poems, participating in every school and church play, and leading school committees to becoming a quiet and socially awkward person. You see, English wasn't the only thing holding me back. My body wasn't used to the amount of processed foods I became exposed to during the first year I lived in Chicago. August flew by before I realized it, and the fall and winter took over. The sunlight was practically gone, and the night arrived in mid-afternoon. Back home, I used the afternoons to run around and play with friends. That part of my day became non-existent. Needless to say, I gained lots of weight and became even more insecure.

Along with the extra pounds, I was carrying a much heavier load. At the age of five, I had been sexually molested by an older girl. The abuse went on for a long time. The psychological damage hit home in my early to mid-teen years. Aside from the embarrassment, guilt, and shame I lived in for several years, I didn't know whether I liked boys or girls. I could never talk about what took place with anyone for a very long time. I didn't even have the courage to tell my mother. This older girl was a relative; a relative whom my parents trusted and treated as a daughter.

Fortunately, a youth group I belonged to as a teenager became a safe haven for me. Through talking and sharing my experience with other people, I began to heal. I realized I wasn't the only one to go through such an ordeal. I also realized there were plenty of people willing to help me, and that what happened was NOT my fault. Most importantly, I began to accept who I was and who I was becoming. It took a while to get to that point. Much later, I also realized that the 'older' girl who was my abuser wasn't much older than me. I also wondered what abuse she went through and if she ever had the chance to heal.

That acceptance of myself helped me in the years to come. I graduated high school with honors and as a co-valedictorian of my class. I thought I had it all figured out. My plan was to attend college, study abroad, learn three more languages, and become an international business woman. The fact that my parents could not afford to pay for my college education was never an obstacle. I was going to obtain my degree no matter what.

MAKING CHANGES

Then the first year of college came. It was a tough one. I went from a school of 250 students to a school with a few thousand students. I got pregnant that year too, and became overwhelmed with tiredness, school studies, and after school work to pay for my tuition.

My plans were altered. It was time to adjust and make the best of my new situation. I took a leave of absence from school from April to June. My son was just under five months old when I went back to school as a full-time student in September. Now, I had to work to pay tuition and support my family. Working part time wasn't an option.

I must admit, being a full-time student while working a full-time job and raising a baby was incredibly challenging. I had countless sleepless nights, a couple of D's and extremely high levels of caffeine in my system along with an ulcer, very few friends, and no social life. Sometimes people ask me, how did you do it? The truth is, I never stopped to think about how challenging it was or how much farther I had to go. I had no time for any of that. All I did was work, study, and focus on my child. Nothing else mattered. There were days I could barely function, days when I was beyond exhausted and emotionally drained. There are plenty of days I don't even remember.

Deep down I refused to become one more negative statistic. I was determined to be the first in my family to obtain a college degree and have a corporate job. I didn't exactly know what it would be, but I knew a college education was important for me. Somehow, I found the time and energy to take workshops in public speaking and leadership development. Through time, I learned to accept and make the best of having a foreign accent. I realized I was my biggest critic and I had to learn to be kind to myself. The process of forgiving myself and dealing with the guilt of the forgotten memories during my son's childhood came later and that's a separate chapter.

CONFIDENCE RETURNED

It took me six years to obtain my bachelor's degree, but I did it. I felt accomplished and relieved. I know that phase of my life would have been even more challenging had I not had the support of my immediate family. I'm eternally grateful to my mother for always making education a priority in our family, to my father for instilling in me a good work ethic and to my siblings who became young parents with me.

Many more people played a significant role in my life and made me a stronger person. I'm thankful to them as well. I have been fortunate to have a strong support system since early on and it has become much stronger in the latter part of my life. I am now married and have two more wonderful kids. My daughter is eight and my son is five. My husband has become a strong pillar in my life. When I begin to doubt myself or become overconfident, he helps me to look at things from a different perspective. He often challenges me to take the next step and always seems to find the way and the time to support my ideas, projects, and adventures. I am eternally grateful our paths crossed when they did.

The journey to feeling invincible and fearless once again has come gradually. Overcoming childhood traumas, getting an education, working out and losing the extra pounds has helped me tremendously. However, what has made a true difference has been embracing my vulnerabilities, accepting them, and forgiving myself. Silencing the noise around me and within me has become a daily habit along with gratitude. Listening to uplifting music, reading spiritual growth books, and surrounding myself with positive people have made a world of difference in my life. Yes, there are days when despair and fear peek through, but a quick glance or thought of my amazing children is enough to bring me peace.

My daughter's relentless determination, my older son's sense of justice and my little one's kindness bring me infinite joy. I have a strong sense of responsibility towards them. I want to create a better world for them and the young generations emerging. I want to give them the tools they need to stand for justice, compassion, and to revolutionize the status quo.

REFLECTION

1. What can you do to be kind to yourself today?
2. What activities can help you heal and overcome your past?
3. What factors have diminished your confidence over the years? How can you reverse them?

BIOGRAPHY

Angelica Monroy was born in the U.S., raised in Mexico and permanently relocated to Chicago when she was 15. She was the first in her family to receive a college degree, earning a B.A in International Studies with a minor in management from DePaul University in 2002. Just after graduation, Angelica joined Banco Popular as a manager and began a 16-year corporate career. She most recently participated as a volunteer with "Mujeres Latinas En Accion", which provides assistance and council to victims of domestic violence and as a board member of "Corazon a Corazon", which serves the Latino communities in South Chicago. She is a past board member and current committee member of "Latinas on the Plaza", a professional Latina women's group.

In 2014, Angelica left her successful career in banking and became a franchise owner at British Swim School. She and her business partner operate more than ten pools in the Chicago Suburbs and are currently in the process of building their own. Angelica received the Daily Herald Business Ledger Influential Women In Business Award in November of 2015. She currently

 resides in Westchester, IL, with her husband Diego, and her three children Ricardo (18), Valeria (8), and Jacob (5).

Angelica Monroy
angelica.monroy@britishswimschool.com

Yaneth Medina

"Feeling successful is essential. Set mini-goals to get to your larger goal."

The path to self-discovery starts at a very young age. We learn from our experiences and if done correctly, we can create anything we want. It's interesting how events in our lives impact us in one way or another. As I reminisce about my childhood, I remember how happy I was. My parents created an environment of positivity and a notion that hard work and dedication will pay off in everything that we do. They taught my siblings and I that we can do anything we set our minds to, despite living in a country that was so different from home. Nonetheless, this was never an obstacle for them. Siempre luchaban por lo mejor para su familia!!

SETTING GOALS

As the oldest of three children, I was the one that experienced the first of many uncomfortable situations. I was the one that entered grade school without knowing one word of English. I couldn't speak or read it at all. To this day, it still amazes me how quickly I adapted to the American culture and the English language.

I grew up in Des Plaines, Illinois where only a small percentage of the town's population was Hispanic. When compared to larger cities like Chicago, Elgin, and Aurora, we were the minority. Certain events really impacted me as I grew up. I was part of the small group of kids that were separated daily from our regular class and it wasn't fun.

It never really hit me until later in life that this created a notion of – "Why?" Why was it that we (the Spanish-speaking kids) were being removed from the rest? It was then that I discovered I didn't want to be judged or removed for not being fluent in the English language; I wanted to stay with the rest of my class and be just like everyone else. I was no different than everyone else. This was my first discovery of how to subconsciously empower myself to improve.

Growing up as a Latina and being a first-generation kid in the United States wasn't easy. There are many cultural differences between the Hispanic household and the American household. When I was a kid, I had a hard time embracing this and often struggled with being different. Kids always want to feel part of a group and not be the outcast in school.

I still remember how "The Green Eggs and Ham Day" impacted me as a child. My kindergarten teacher, Mrs. Sorensen, gathered all of us together and was going to give us a snack. My classmates were all excited and couldn't wait to see what was to come. She surprised us by telling us that we were having "green eggs and ham" just like the book by Dr. Seuss. Everyone screamed with joy and I was a bit disgusted. There was no way that I was going to eat "a green egg" much less "green ham." Yuck! How could everyone eat this? It was not until I was much older that I realized how this life event influenced me. As I recall this situation, I realize how unguarded I was with this type of new experience. This was one of those instances when I really wish I had been more open to change.

I grew up, my confidence continued to grow and I was starting to believe that everything was meant to be. My parents had sacrificed themselves to raise us in America and I could not let them down. Being on the honor roll was always my goal. Going to school and doing my homework was something that I enjoyed. I wanted to make my parents proud and give them the honor of seeing their daughter get a high school diploma. My parents had no means for a higher education in Mexico. They came from families where they had to work at a very young age to put food on the table. Both of them only attended school until the fourth grade. Yet, they are among the smartest people I know and have beautiful handwriting.

I pushed myself in school and always strived to get good grades. My goal at that time was to become a teacher. Everything was perfect and I was happy as can be. Just like any other teen, interest in school wasn't my only priority. Going to high school really opened my eyes. Yes, getting good grades was super important but so was fitting in with everyone else.

DISTRACTION FROM GOALS

Long story short, there were distractions that kept me from getting my high school diploma and attending college. My whole world changed in a matter of seconds when I was told that I was pregnant and would be having a baby in the fall. I recall hearing the news and being scared and disappointed with myself because of the pain I caused my parents. It was a tough couple of months. I couldn't look at my parents, especially my dad. I knew that I had broken his heart. Despite causing so much pain and disappointment, my parents and family gave me support.

Differences were set aside and it was now time to persevere. (You can say that this was when I first realized the power that I had within myself.) With the love and support of my family, I was blessed with a beautiful son, Raul, in the fall. It was a blessing to have delivered a perfectly healthy boy. My motherly instincts kicked in as soon as I held my baby boy in my arms. Growing up, I had loved kids and always babysat for friends and family. My little brother was born when I was 11 and I took care of him just like he was my own son.

I would be lying if I said that it was an easy transition. It wasn't. I was a teen mother taking care of an infant while still managing high school homework, working, and dealing with a new formal relationship. My boyfriend and father of my son moved in, and my life changed in a matter of seconds. As I recall my past, I don't think I ever realized what could happen if I had a baby. So many girls in my school were moms and it seemed like it was nothing new.

The struggle to take care of myself with all my demands continued. My parents stated that they would help me with whatever it took to graduate high school. After I had my son and was able to return to school, I felt a need to excel. I was not going to allow myself to fail at this. I had to make my parents proud. And so I continued to focus on school and as a result, I earned my first 4.0 GPA despite my circumstances. I owe all of this to the fire that automatically ignited inside me, once I set my mind to it. You see, we all have this within ourselves; you just need to realize it.

Making minimum wage on a part-time job as a new mother was not making ends meet. I then made a conscious decision to graduate early from high school and try to get hired as a teller. One of my friends had told me the bank was hiring, so I committed myself to getting the job. I set my mind to it. It took several phone calls and much perseverance to get hired, but I did it.

I started to work full time in banking and then I learned that in the fall, I was expecting again. It was a nice, yet scary surprise. How was I going to do this with two kids, a job and a family? My goal of going to college and getting a degree was fading away. Coming from an atmosphere of positivity, I stopped thinking like this and decided to move forward and believe that this was meant to be. There was a reason this was happening.

CREATING NEW GOALS

That September, I had my other son, Angel. This time the

delivery was easier and everything seemed to be going much better. I had this! And so I returned to work as soon as I could.

For one reason or another, I enjoyed working in the banking industry. The notion of being able to help people gave me much joy. I had discovered a passion of mine. I found an awesome daycare for my kids and I was able to return to work on a full-time basis.

During my first year in banking, I quickly discovered that I was bored being a teller. Although I enjoyed the environment and the people I worked for, I felt unchallenged in the role. I then applied to be in Operations and got the job as the IRA coordinator. I learned so much.

Ultimately, though, I didn't last too long in this department and ended up as the receptionist for the personal banking department. I loved this! My next goal was to become a personal banker and that is what I did. I learned as much as I could and when a position opened up, I applied and was hired.

Working for a community bank gave me the experience I needed to be a successful banker; I was someone who could help people with their finances. I kept confirming the passion that I had to help people and how good it felt. Despite working full time and being a full-time mom and wife, I continued my education. My family helped me continue my dream. The evening classes at a local community college were perfect! Years later, I even reached my goal of finishing my B. S. in Finance from Roosevelt University.

I was always very busy with family, work, and school.

Eventually, I decided to take on a management role in banking. I was a successful banker and I wanted to help others as well. And this is exactly what I did. I think about this now and people ask me all the time, how did I do it? My answer to them is, "I don't know. I just did it. It was the power and drive that I had to push myself and be successful. Failing was not an option. I also think that loving what you do is key."

Today, I can tell you that I continue to tap into the power that I hold. We all have the capability of being who we want to be. You just need to believe in yourself and set goals. Feeling successful is essential and this is why you need to set mini-goals to get to your larger goal. Today, I am mom with three wonderful boys. My oldest boys are both in college pursuing their careers and my little boy is in grade school.

I'm proud to say that I am still in banking! My work now entails being on a senior management team. I continue to help people with their financial needs and employee development. My advice to you is to follow your dreams, discover your power, believe in yourself and let go! You will see the magic.

REFLECTION

1. What power do you hold that can be unlocked?

2. A positive attitude can be a powerful thing. What aspect of your life is hardest to stay positive about and how might you find that positivity?

3. What small goals can you set along the way to reach your larger goals?

BIOGRAPHY

Yaneth Medina serves as a Senior Vice President of Retail Banking and Head of Retail for a Chicago land-based financial institution. Yaneth has more than 20 years of experience in retail banking, relationship building, workplace culture, and coaching and mentoring. She wears many hats and serves on many internal committees, including business development, compliance, and employee recognition. She also sits on a couple retail advisory boards at the corporate level.

Yaneth's strong work ethic and integrity have helped her achieve in her career. She is also viewed by colleagues as a supportive member of the management team and she understands the value of promoting and inspiring a positive culture in which everyone can thrive.

She also dedicates her time to serving several organizations in the local area. Currently, she is the board president for Centro De Informacion of Elgin, IL and a board member for the Elgin Area Chamber of Commerce. She also serves on committees for other local organizations.

Yaneth's family consists of her three wonderful boys, her parents, and her brother and sister. They have been her inspiration!

Yaneth Medina
Medinay427@gmail.com
(847) 812-7859

TAKING RISKS, MAKING DECISIONS, AND REAPING WHAT YOU SOW

Lida Esperanza Garzón

"To receive, let go."

I lost my mother when I was 11. After watching her die at the age of 42 from brain cancer, a suffering phase that lasted eight years, I experienced a feeling of forced detachment for the first time in my life. My mother's death awakened a vital force within that refused to allow life to make decisions for me anymore. Thus, I began a life of adventure and taking risks. At 16, I left home and embarked on a journey to take comprehensive leadership training for young people at the Youth Center in Colombia. This wonderful place opened my eyes to the horizons of unimaginable possibilities and strengthened the foundation of values and principles I received at home.

During the next five years, I ventured to live alone with limited financial resources and worked continuously with no vacation time or rest in order to save enough money for a private college education. Between the ages of 17 and 19, I got the opportunity to work in private companies where I held various positions from receptionist to sales representative. This learning experience taught me how to deal with organizational environments, develop the habit of saving and administer my personal finances. Every day was highly productive as I developed discipline while seeking my dream of becoming a professional industrial engineer.

This goal was somewhat against the wishes of my father, who supported me in my studies, though he feared for my safety as I pursued my career path in a big city like Bogotá. In unfamiliar surroundings, I would be vulnerable and unprotected. Aware of his concern, I learned how to deal with dangerous situations by holding on to the idea that God and my mother were taking care of me from above. This belief gave me a lot of confidence. Weekend visits to my father calmed his fears and I chose to narrate the good while casually sharing my difficult situations as anecdotes. I had learned to laugh at my experiences and to value each challenge that I overcame with the certainty that in the end, everything would turn out well. I also learned to have a good attitude and to look at life with humor.

Therefore, fear does not limit me, but rather, it drives me. Challenges keep me focused on learning and growing as a professional, living a formative experience in different organizational fields, achieving leadership positions and excelling as Production Engineer and Director of Human Resources. My understanding of human nature and the need to align human talent with the strategic plan of the business provided certain clarity about my professional vocation, which led me into my second career as a coach. Coaching is my passion and through it I have experienced the satisfaction of making my own decisions and accomplishing most of my mission in life. I have lived in a continuum of risks that have produced fruits of unlimited growth.

BREAKING OFF CHAINS TO LIVE IN FREEDOM

It was the summer of 2012 in Lima, Peru. I was 37 years old and in my eighth year as an executive coach. I remember getting back to the hotel room, ready to rest after one of my typical, intense and challenging days with my executive coaching clients at a very prestigious organization where I had created strong bonds of commitment and trust during my professional relationship.

My smile of satisfaction disappeared as I gazed into the mirror, seeing my tired face and finding myself alone, once again, in this continuum of tireless travels throughout South America. I initiated a dialogue about love with myself and as I did, a great moment of clarity opened up in my heart. At the same time, I wondered how good of a coach I could be to myself. Immediately, I had a vision of two possible scenarios for my personal and professional future.

The first scenario was to maintain the same pace at which I was living my life. I was then headed for a future filled with greater experience, recognition and professional status, but also exhaustion, old age, and loneliness. The loneliness in particular was the saddest prospect for me. The second scenario was a vision free of anything I was currently experiencing, where I saw myself daring to embrace a radical detachment to release all the bonds that held me in a comfortable, professional zone of "success," but which neglected my fulfillment as a woman. I saw myself free of business trips and assignments, yet established in a place with greater stability and prosperity.

With determination, joy, and impetus I made a radical decision to let go of all existing security and instead take a path toward an encounter with my own heart, a path that I envisioned would be far from familiar, everyday surroundings. In just five months, I managed to finish up with my clients and said my goodbyes to colleagues and staff with great sadness. Still very determined to follow the desires of my heart, so strong was my resolution that I even declined an attractive job offer that my clients' company proposed with the hopes of retaining my services. In July 2012, I placed all of my material goods where they might be useful and experienced the joy of living with light baggage, a heart full of dreams and a feeling of spreading my new wings and taking off toward freedom.

Five months later, this moment of truth landed me in the city of Chicago to experience an intense period I like to call my "sabbatical year". In reality, it was more of a true spiritual retreat that allowed me the time to rethink my future. Detachment for me is something extremely important in life situations that I do not have control over such as, the death of my mother, being unemployed for almost six months, and the end of a relationship that promised marriage. These are three examples of the importance of radical acceptance - when things are not in your hands and you cannot change them, they require true detachment. The more I give importance to overcoming situations of grief, loss and depression, the sooner I feel that I can move on to the next level. That scenario I described in the Lima hotel has more to it. The only lasting relationship I was in for the months I was there had ended. I was with him for three years and was certain we would get married. Going through the five stages of grief (denial, anger, depression, negotiation and acceptance) required my attention to give outlet to emotions like guilt and sadness and work with forgiveness in order to transform them and heal.

That is how traveling to Chicago and giving myself that time to let go of my job security and career success was part of my healing process. My own story teaches me to give importance to every situation in life. I love to talk to my own heart, to know the message behind the beliefs, fears, desires, skills and how all of these constitute the things that I am, since they all have an impact on the near future. The epiphany at the Lima hotel and the decision to drop everything was an empowering event and example of a loss that was not out of my control. On the contrary, it was a conscious decision. Knowing that there are things that life takes away and others in which I choose to let go, empowers me and gives me confidence to keep moving toward my ideals. Staying in the comfort zone sometimes makes us feel confined. What is important is learning and moving forward to achieve what we want. To receive, I had to let go. That is why I consider detachment a fundamental tool in my life, to walk free of any heavy baggage and be opened to receive the good that comes my way.

I eventually decided upon a plan to return to my home

country, Colombia, and open Hope Coaching. Just a month before I was scheduled to depart, I met Marcos Montiel, a persistent, intelligent, lover of freedom and a dreamer troubled by the development of Latinos in the United States. He was eager to discover new options that would allow people to fulfill their dreams of coming to this country. He is a financial advisor and now coach. We met at a perfect time where I felt peaceful, not looking to fill any emotional space in my life and willing to accept unconditionally with love everything new that God brought before me. Marcos and I share simplicity and transparency without pretenses, which has made it easier to flow together with love and freedom. In February 2013, we began a generous, open and honest engagement and spent two and a half years in the freest relationship I have ever had. We got married in October 2015. Today I feel fulfilled, with open arms. I am practicing acceptance and detachment, which has made for a very healthy relationship and has filled us with renewed love every day. Perhaps because we both learned to love like this, I love to live in the present and as his wife, I thank him for it.

THE FORCE THAT DRIVES AND INSPIRES

Undoubtedly, decisions like those I have made are possible when we have allies we can count on, who love us and believe in us. I believe deeply in the creative and supreme power of God that lives in my heart; I believe that being connected with His omnipotent force was the best thing that ever happened to me. It was He who opened up a wonderful scenario in this country through my cousin, Nestor Torres, a Catholic priest I have always admired and respected, and with whom I have shared my deep reflections of life. Today, thanks to him, I have many friends and a large spiritual family. My gratitude also goes to the many people who, with their love and support, have accompanied me in this transformative stage. In addition, my mother's spiritual presence is a driving force that pushes and inspires me, as is the constant love of my father, who learned to trust my decisions and support me across the distance with his prayers and affection. Finally, the staff of Coaching For Wellness, LLC with which I currently work, is definitely inspiring and the perfect complement to my life, for they allow me to serve through coaching and to achieve a state of complete satisfaction.

Relationships are maintained when there is a bond and a connection with no attachment. After three years of absence, my clients have contacted me once again, expressing their desire to continue with my services. Today, I offer my virtual executive coaching services to corporate clients in South America from the comfort of my home. I also dedicate myself to the exciting task of forming professional coaches from my role as mentor and trainer coach. I am a member of the International Coach Federation, aspiring to complete my MCC credential this year. My current interest is focused on working with women like me who dream of feeling fulfillment in their lives and together with my spouse, supporting engaged and married couples, and families by promoting unity, love and communication.

REFLECTION

1. What are your biggest attachments? How would you be without them?

2. What is the force that drives you forward?

3. How light and detached are you to be able to receive new gifts that life has in store for you?

BIOGRAPHY

Lida is a Colombian woman who is passionate about coaching education. She is a certified professional coach from Coaching For Wellness and a master coach in process, with over 11 years of experience. As a coach facilitator and mentor, Lida trains individuals in the coaching profession to be life and corporate coaches, as well as spiritual and team coaches. She currently specializes in forming professional Hispanic coaches in several U.S. locations and in Spanish-speaking countries around the world. Lida prides herself on her emotional intelligence and assertive communication which helps her build rapport with clients and her students at Coaching for Wellness LLC, a pioneer in the Latin American market.

Prior to working with Coaching for Wellness, Lida developed her coaching career at American College of Interpersonal Development, where she promoted executive coaching in Colombia, Venezuela, Ecuador and Peru. Lida has a degree in industrial engineering with experience in production and also, in human resources.

Lida Esperanza Garzón, CPC
lida@coachingforwellness.com
(224) 227-8275

BACK TO THE ROOTS

Diane Luna Martin

"My passion is to bridge success across all borders."

I want to open with a personal anecdote of a recent trip to Ecuador – my parents' home country - which reminded me of my roots. My mother always said, "It's important to know where you come from, to know where you're headed to next and which values are at the core of your success."

It was a special day for my Great Aunt "Tia" Teo. Not only was her 100th birthday coming up, but she had also heard rumors that I might be travelling to Ecuador all the way from California to celebrate her.

When I finally walked into the room, the surprised look on her beautiful face showed delight and disbelief, and that joy was already worth the trip. I smiled at my dear inspirational aunt. How could I miss it? It wasn't every day you turned 100! I consider my aunt to have been very instrumental in my life. Tia Teo was my grandmother's sister, and someone who always encouraged and believed in me. She was an elementary school teacher, and spent much of her life educating others, even giving of her time to help those in prison.

Born in New York City of Ecuadorean parents, I spoke

English at school and Spanish at home. When I was young, we returned to live in Ecuador where I attended high school, and it was Tia Teo who helped me become a better speaker in Spanish. In many ways, she illustrated the foundation of my family and the deep belief in education and compassion, both so important in helping me become the person I am today. Seeing her again just made me realize how strongly these values and principles have formed my family and me.

AN ORIGINAL UPBRINGING

My family was like a Latin version of the Brady bunch. My mom came to the marriage with two sons and my father brought a daughter. Then came me—the surprise baby and product of their love.

We weren't a wealthy family but we were close and happy together. My much older siblings willingly took partial responsibility in my raising as they loved, encouraged and nurtured me. We were a diverse family, with dramatically different viewpoints but we had a loyalty and bond to each other that has indelibly shaped my personal and professional development. We were raised to compete and succeed, but my parents fostered a family belief in collaboration, respect and equality. Everyone could "make it happen" but we were to help each other succeed too.

As a child, I was always a creative problem solver and still am today. From the time I started to walk (or rather, climb up on precarious places to see what was on the other side) I wanted to see what else there was—explore the possibilities. Because of my natural curiosity, I loved school, learning and languages. Living each day speaking both English and Spanish developed my interest in the etymology of words.

By the age of 10, my parents decided to move back to Ecuador. My brothers and sister, who were always good role models for me, remained in the U.S. to attend college, while I was to attend high school in Ecuador.

There, education differed greatly from the U.S. Basically, in your sophomore year, you choose one of three academic tracks: social studies, towards a career in social sciences or art; chemistry/biology towards a career in medicine; or physics/math towards a career in business. By that time, I had discovered I was very good in lab work, so I decided medicine would be my calling, and potentially become a surgeon. I even had the chance to teach basic health and wellness to the underserved communities in Quito.

Chemistry fascinated me and I found anatomy/physiology easy to memorize all the material. It was dissection that hindered my progress: I would put the knife to the specimen and faint dead away every time. So much for becoming a surgeon!

I bounced back from that, refocused my career planning and – as it would turn out later - pursued health care in a different way. I chose to attend university in the U.S. and enrolled at Barry University in Miami, near my brothers. The day I graduated with a B.A. in Public Relations in 2001 was such a proud one for my family, in the U.S. as well as Ecuador. They encouraged me to go on to pursue an MBA, but I was yearning to learn more about the world with first-hand real experiences, through travel and maybe the corporate world as well.

So I accepted a position with Dignity Health, one of the largest, most successful health care systems in the U.S. It was located in California and during my seven years there, I was promoted several times while working in their communications and marketing department. Still, I felt there was more I could do.

A CURIOUS CALLING

In 2006, I was ready to enter graduate school at nearby University of Redlands. All was going well, until tragedy struck. My mother passed away unexpectedly. I was devastated and didn't know if I could keep going. But my mother, like my dad and siblings, constantly supported and encouraged my educational pursuits. "Avanza, mi hija, avanza!" she would tell me, which means, "keep moving forward!" How could I let her down now? It is when life hits you hardest that you discover most about yourself and your inner strength.

In 2008, I completed my MBA in Global Business in her honor and I'm proud to be the first woman in my family with an advanced degree. My family members were immensely proud, and I knew I could not have done it without their constant love and support.

What next? I had learned a lot in the corporate world and felt I had the background and abilities to start my own consultancy. My curious and spontaneous personality had contributed to an eclectic resume including brand strategist for health care start-ups, mid-level and large companies. In addition, there was a need in the market for an experienced healthcare system specific marketing consultant. It was 2010 and the recession was in full swing. Many hospitals were restructuring to improve patient care and delivery. This translated into an opportunity for me. So, with all the courage I could muster, I left my job and opened my doors as a consultant.

What helped me succeed on my own? I would say it was my natural conviction to discover more, my love of learning and my ability to quickly seek out new opportunities with integrity. As a consultant, I would have to uncover every new client's corporate story, including their successes; pains, challenges, goals, etc. to help define, design and deliver on a strategy and their brand promise. If they felt they had an obstacle to overcome, I would ask "why" until we uncovered the solutions together. Then I could develop the "how" to take action and meet their objectives.

By 2013 the opportunity of a lifetime was presented when Stanford University's Health Care system contracted me in the marketing and communications department to lead every facet of a product launch and branding program, from determining positioning, naming, competitive analysis, feature prioritization, external communication and strategic alliances. For me, it was a dream job!

A BRIDGE ACROSS BORDERS

Because I was born into the melting pot of New York

City, I thought I understood what diversity was, but only on my extensive trips throughout the world I learned what true diversity meant.

These experiences widened my cultural and social horizon, which in turn have helped me become a better consultant because I improved my social and communication skills. In graduate school, I traveled to Hong Kong and Tokyo as we studied how China's economy was changing from a communist to a capitalist model. Travel through Latin America, Asia, Europe and Turkey has showed me how beneficial our cultural differences can be and how many business opportunities abound.

Conventional political wisdom tells us that our differences may divide us because they often breed fear and cause conflict. However, I believe we are living in the golden age of understanding diversity and collaboration. Studies have shown that profitability increases when diverse groups are encouraged to collaborate more. If a company wants to outstrip the competition, it needs to influence how people can productively work together with various backgrounds. That's when I realized that the cultural differences in the U.S. are an advantage for me and that I can accomplish more here. I was sure my status as a Latina, born in New York, would give me an edge and could be an asset for any partnership.

America is a more tolerant, inclusive society where people are taken at face value. Latinas can be empowered based on the intelligence and value they can add. As a Latina with the required educational qualifications that are needed to compete in our society, I can work and live on a level playing field like any other woman in this country. In addition to that, my Latin American heritage taught me compassion and the ability to care, care for your family, care for your clients, and care for yourself without compromise.

My world travel has made me a more understanding, perceptive person at work as well as in my personal life. I am able to gain peoples' trust and understand their reservations because I understand their origins through my experiences with other cultures. Instead of generalizing a culture or group because it is easy, it is far better to understand a culture by answering, "why are they doing it this way?"

I look around me and I am excited to see Latinas taking charge of their own destiny now more than ever before. I strive to be a positive voice for others and challenge the role they play in society. The communities that we live and work in may be unaware of the contributions of Latinas, but also uninformed of Latin culture and the positive impacts we have made throughout history. Often people mistakenly limit their perception to the nearest Spanish-speaking country. Ecuador, for example, is only one Latin American country of 41 nations that range from small islands to large economies, with a wide diversity of millions of Spanish-speaking people from different backgrounds!

We all have a unique origin that we bring to the table and when we let it shine in our everyday endeavors, we can change how people see our culture and us in society. I encourage you to proudly infuse your origin and your multi-cultural experience into everything you do. Whatever your dreams are or wherever your curiosity may lead you, take your essence with you. For me, my essence goes back to my family and education, which centers me to add value and bridge success across all borders.

Currently, I am in Palo Alto, at the heart of Silicon Valley, where digital innovation and diverse solutions meet to explore possibilities for the wellbeing of patient care delivery. I don't know what the future holds as new opportunities arise, but I would be excited to meet and work with inspirational Latinas to create something that improves healthcare, technology and education initiatives for everyone. I'm curious to find out what that will be.

REFLECTION

1. How have your "roots" helped you become the person you are today?

2. What two things motivate you most to succeed?

3. How has curiosity served you in your life?

BIOGRAPHY

Diane Luna Martin is a native New Yorker and the daughter of Ecuadorean parents. She is an award-winning executive with more than 12 years experience and a track record in building successful branding, marketing and communications strategies for healthcare start-ups, mid-level and large companies. Diane has worked with innovative partners that include Stanford Health Care, Dignity Health, Cardinal Health and Abbott.

As a child, Diane spoke Spanish at home and English at school, helping to develop a passion for the etymology of words. She earned a B.A. in Public Relations from Barry University and an MBA in Global Business from the University of Redlands while focusing on healthcare operations and Asian markets. Her studies abroad ignited her passion for world perspectives as she completed coursework in Tokyo and Hong Kong and later enjoyed travels throughout Latin America, Asia, Europe and Turkey.

Diane Luna Martin
Connect on LinkedIn
(951) 217-6011

MY CHILDHOOD, MY RESILIENCE

Nydia Monarrez

"Follow your dreams despite what other people think, and work towards them every day."

I was born and raised in Monterrey, Nuevo León Mexico, the third of four daughters. My parents had a very dysfunctional marriage. My dad (R.I.P.) was an alcoholic who never recognized it. Most weekends my dad got drunk and fought with my mom. Bad language and psychological abuse were a weekend thing. Many times my dad would try to hit my mom, and my older sister would try to stop it. He would drive the car when he was drunk with all of us on board. It truly was a miracle that we never had a car accident, because my parents would fight in the car too.

My dad use to carry a gun and sleep with it under the mattress for "protection purposes." Sometimes, he would shoot it into the air or through the window just to show us how "cool" it sounded. There were holes in several screens around the house. One time, the bullets went through one of the walls in the living room and had to be repainted to cover the damage.

Finances and money were another issue. My mom was always doing or selling something to generate extra income for clothing and vacations, because my dad's salary was never enough.

I remember a time when my dad had lost his job, my mom's business was not doing very well, and I was looking for loose change in the drawers to help my mom afford to buy a quart of milk because my youngest sister needed some and there was none in the fridge.

I remember begging my parents to get divorced. I thought it would have been easier and healthier for all of us, but I guess the custom to stay married was stronger than anything else.

I finally stopped judging them years ago because, who am I to judge? They both loved me and my sisters to death. Unfortunately, they just didn't know how to raise us better.

LETTING GO

I could share even more traumatic tales from my childhood, but that is not the purpose of my story. However, as a result of my background, I grew up with a lot of physical, emotional, and psychological insecurities. I felt "less than" and believed that I didn't deserve wellness, peace, abundance, security, and happiness. Instead, I developed a hub of emotions like embarrassment, madness, fear, frustration, impotency, sadness, and courage in many aspects of myself.

As you can imagine, experiencing all those feelings at such an early stage in life was truly painful and overwhelming. Unfortunately, many of those events were repeated during my teens and twenties. Through my faith, teachings, courses, and workshops from different sources and above all, internal examination, I learned to overcome many of the insecurities we tend to carry with us as human beings. I am not saying that I am done with my personal issues, not at all. However, I have learned to laugh about myself, my insecurities and my crazy thoughts about life in general. I have learned it is smarter to go with the flow, letting the past go to focus on future goals. I also stopped arguing and complaining about my childhood, since that is a fight that I will never win, simply because it is over.

In Mexico, Quinceañera is celebrated with a big party. In my case, I got a great trip to Disneyland and Las Vegas instead. The trip was amazing, and I came back home with a bunch of brochures, and information from the theme parks, hotels, places I had visited, etc. and told my Mom she had to organize a tour to those places. One of my Mom's businesses at that time was organizing tours to vacation spots in Mexico and the U.S. The next year, she took a group to Disneyland/Vegas and the year after, to Disney World in Orlando, Florida where I learned about a job opportunity.

LESSONS ON THE CORPORATE LADDER

I got my very first job at McDonald's when I was 16 years old, right after finishing high school. Originally, I was going to quit and attend college in the fall but I was having so much fun working there, I ended up staying for a whole year. Within a few months, I was promoted to trainer and I learned a lot about processes, quality control, customer care, and human resources.

While in college studying communications with a focus on public relations and organizational development, I had some work experiences. I moved to Texas before starting my fifth semester, in order to study English as a second language. I lived with an American family and worked as nanny for one year. After my return to Mexico to finish school, I worked a full-time job as a director's assistant. However, I knew Disney had a program for hiring students from Mexico and other countries to work as cultural representatives at their respective pavilions at the EPCOT theme park. In my last year of school, I applied for a position. They offered me a one-year contract in the EPCOT Mexican pavilion. I started work right after graduating from the Universidad Autónoma de Nuevo León.

Thus began one of the most magical experiences of my career. Working for Disney changed my perspective on life. I learned a lot about marketing, customer satisfaction, and Disney traditions. Imagine sharing an apartment with five girls from different countries, with five different types of cuisine to taste. I became a happy foodie! Because contracts started on different months for each of us during my time at Disney, I had thirteen different roommates from nine different countries.

At the end of my contract, I took a final trip to Europe for three weeks with my cousin Adriana. We had a blast! I strongly advise you to invest in trips around your state, across the country, and internationally. It is really great food for your soul, an awesome source of inspiration for your goals and dreams, and an eye opener in terms of life's perspective. I could write a book about all my great memories working with Mickey Mouse, but again, this is not the purpose of my story.

I returned home to reality and looked for a "real job". I went to my very first interview, and was hired the same day by a financial institution. I received a very good salary. I worked there for four years in several positions, rising to Corporate Sales Manager, and leading a team of 90 people. During that time, I met "Mr. Right", my wonderful husband, Roldan Vazquez.

I joined a larger financial corporation and worked there for six years, mainly in sales and promotion as I got married and became mother to two "one of a kind" kids.

And then another great opportunity knocked my door.

CHANGES AND THE U.S.

I had never stopped dreaming about returning to the U.S. as a recruited hire in a full-time, corporate job with paid relocation expenses. I have always believed in the force of the subconscious mind. That dream was always there, and I thought about it regularly, so guess what? It happened to me! Long story short, I was chosen to work on an initiative to reach the Latino Market in the U.S. I relocated to Florida, which allowed my husband to work at his company's headquarters in Tampa. We moved in December of 2009. Relocating was demanding, and my new position as a Multicultural Sales Support Manager was very challenging. Getting my Series 6 license (a must for my new position on finances) was overwhelming, but I did it!

My life right after moving to U.S. was full of learning experiences and wouldn't have been possible without the wonderful support system of my sister, my in-laws, my mom, new friends, and several stay-in nannies. Keep in mind that you can't do everything by yourself and you can count on other people's help to reach your goals and dreams.

I had been working at the company for almost two years when they went through an IPO (Initial Public Offer) and laid off the multicultural team along with many other people. I was in shock! Tears came to my eyes. I recall thinking, "This is not happening. You don't bring several families from different countries and let them go in less than two years." I went home and told my husband. He was in shock too. During the following weeks, I started to think that everything happens for a reason. I just couldn't see that reason yet.

I went through all the cycles of loss. I was mad, sad, depressed, happy, confused etc. I knew I wanted to work, but I didn't feel like going back to the corporate world again. Finally, after some introspection, I told myself, "Whatever you do now is going to be fun and you will enjoy doing it regardless of the salary."

When I was a child, I wanted to be an actress and speak in front of an audience or behind a microphone, but never expressed it. The only time I did it, was when I was in fourth grade. My teacher gave me a disappointed look and said, "No Nydia, don't do that." My heart shrank and I put my dream in a drawer, and never told anyone else about it. So I thought, that's it! This is what I always wanted to do, and I will do it, even if it seems too late to start!

When I told my husband my decision, he said, "Why

Nydia?" Just tell me why you want to become an actress?"

I replied, "Because I am passionate about being many different people, and still being me. I could be a business woman, a homeless person, a lawyer, a doctor, a mom, a queen, a bitch and everything in between!"

"You are already all that," he replied, and I just laughed.

I knocked on two doors, looking for representation and one of them immediately accepted me and suggested I do lifestyle modeling as well. I went to castings for commercials and found they were looking for real actors, so I started taking acting classes with C.S.A. Kathy Laughlin and got some voiceover training. My kids also got involved in the industry, and even dad help us out with real family gigs.

In the spring of 2014, my husband mentioned a job opportunity in Chicago within the same company, and I immediately said yes. I was ready for a change. We bought our very first home in the U.S., and invested in my career as a Spanish voiceover talent which was beginning to look more like a full-time job. I built a recording studio in the basement of my home, and I am working and improving my craft, taking private lessons with two great coaches: Simone Fojgiel and Alfonso Lugo. Also, I am studying marketing, reading Dan Kennedy's books and implementing Kim Walsh's social media expert strategies to promote my services. As a result, my business is exploding globally, with clients not only in the U.S. but Mexico, South America, Europe, and India.

I invite you to follow your dreams, as I did, despite what

other people think, and work towards them every day. Remember that where there is a will there is a way, period. I feel very fortunate to be able to do what I love for a living, and I have greater goals for my professional future that I can't wait to see become a reality!

I am a work in progress, and always will be, since that is what life is about: endless growing and lessons to learn, while experiencing happiness and joy at the same time.

REFLECTION

1. What is the vision of your ideal life?

2. What do you REALLY want to do in your life? Seriously, what do you want from the bottom of your heart?

3. What can you do every single day to work towards that goal?

BIOGRAPHY

Nydia Monarrez is a top-rated, Spanish voiceover talent and actress. She helps bridge the gap between clients and the Latino community by recording commercials, medical narrations, e-learning, internet, explainer videos and more. Nydia is represented by agents in the industry in major cities like Los Angeles, New York, Chicago, and Atlanta, as well as Florida, Texas and Colorado. She has worked for such notable clients as Disney, McDonald's, Toyota, Blue Cross Blue Shield, and Oxy Clean. She also does on-camera work and lifestyle modeling. Nydia was born and raised in Monterrey, Mexico and lives in Chicago, IL. She has a B.S. in Communications and Public Relations. For more than ten years she worked at ING Financial, most recently as the Multicultural Sales Support Manager. There she helped close millionaire contracts for Retirement Services.

In 1997, Nydia worked at Citibank Mexico and led a 90-person team as the Corporate Sales Manager. Nydia's ultimate goals are to voice a main character for a Disney or Pixar movie, land a leading role in a film and host a television show promoting travel destinations and restaurants. She is married to Roldan and raising two children, Mauricio and Renata.

Nydia Monarrez
nydia.monarrez@gmail.com
(727) 215-4012

ADAPTING TO CHANGE

Guadalupe "Pita" Betancourt

"Success is to be in peace and harmony with yourself, enjoying the moment."

It was one month after arriving in the U.S. I didn't know the language and had no friends or family in the country. I found myself all alone walking the dark corridors of a hospital on a stormy night accompanied by thunder and terrible lightning. For a few seconds, there was a blackout that seemed like an eternity. After the lights returned, I found a guard who told me where the exit was in Spanish. Finally, I reached the parking lot where my husband's vehicle was parked. That night, I would drive for the first time since my husband was inside the hospital after suffering a heart attack.

The heavy rain kept me moving forward and I climbed into the car. When at last I was in the driver's seat, I could not start the engine. I could not even find the buttons to turn on the lights and wipers. I screamed and cried inconsolably until I realized that no one could help me. I was all alone. I breathed deeply and said, "No one is going to help; only you can help you." I have no idea how I got home to the house I shared happily with the man that I chose.

That same night, he had to have emergency surgery. For me, that was a terrible jolt. The idea of building a new life together as a couple was falling apart. The next day he asked me to leave, to go back to Mexico because his illness had no cure. Of course I stayed. I loved him and decided to fight alongside him against his illness.

FOLLOWING THE LOVE

I was born in central Mexico, in the city of San Luis Potosi, a city of over one million inhabitants. My life was very active socially and politically. Almost every day I would attend cultural activities: art films, exhibitions, plays, etc. Also, I participated as an activist in human rights organizations like Navista's Movement and Women for Democracy.

All my life I had lived with my parents. My father was a big influence in my life because he was a noble, righteous and loving being. We were very close, and enjoyed eating and laughing together. From my mother, I learned to save money and fight for my dreams.

Luckily for me, the reality of the work environment is networking; I was able to get a job through my father's relatives. At age 15, I began working to support myself, which is not very common in Mexico. I really enjoyed my job at Banco Del Centro because it gave me independence and the opportunity to travel. I held many positions, but the one I loved the most was as human resources assistant where I selected personnel for the bank branches. In the 11 years I worked there, I visited several states of the Mexican Republic. Even though there were seasons when the job required many extra hours a day, I was easily able to combine my work with social and family life on a regular basis. This way of life filled me with satisfaction and I was at ease with myself. I felt fulfilled because I had control over my life.

Several times, I thought of living outside of San Luis Potosi since I have always enjoyed traveling and meeting people with different perspectives. However, I never thought I would live in the U.S. because its expansionist economic policies do not seem fair to me. I thought I had everything I needed except for one thing--someone who would support me in my goals, listen to me, let me be free and accept me as I was.

I was discouraged when I saw how many of my girlfriends modified their way of being, acting, speaking, and behaving for their partner, rather than just being themselves. I always felt that all human beings should be valued for who they are, and it is a big problem to believe that we should adapt to another person or let them be in control of us. I felt sure of myself, but I always thought I needed someone else with me to be completely happy. Later on in life, I would learn that if I did not love me enough, I could not make anyone else happy. To love others, one has to love oneself.

The universe sent me the love of my current husband, the kind of man I thought I would never find in my lifetime. All the men I had had a relationship with in the past had wanted to restrict my freedom in one way or another. In 1997, I decided to move to Elgin, Illinois, a city of only 100,000.

I was excited to start my married life. I sent boxes with my entire wardrobe by train to America, imagining that my social life would be equal to or even better than it was in Mexico. What I found was the exact opposite. I was living in a small city, with no recreation, that seemed to have a 9 p.m. curfew, even on weekends. The fact that my husband had moved to Elgin just two months before did not help things since we had not made friends there yet.

Worst of all, he had a stroke. It was his second ever, but the first one I had to face with him. Afterward, I would remember that he had told me about a health problem. However, I had never given much thought about it. It also had never occurred to me to dig deeper and find out more.

FACING REALITY

Without family, close friends or the ability to speak or understand English, I became emotionally paralyzed and completely dependent upon my husband. I was literally locked up all day until he returned from work and took me out for a walk (as it is customary to do with your dog). I was so fearful that if I needed anything, like a simple jar of face cream, I had to ask my husband to take me to the store. The salesperson would just smile and talk to him while I felt completely invisible, like nothing at all.

My life felt completely gray, and I dove into a deeper

depression as I thought about the past and how beautiful it would have been to continue living in Mexico. There, I was living with my loving parents and my 18-year-old daughter, Brenda. Although we were very close, and I wished she had come with me, she decided to stay in Mexico to be with my parents, continue college, and be surrounded by her friends.

When I called my family back home they sounded happy. Of course, my parents and my daughter missed me but they were still enjoying life. Mexico was not always an ideal country but people worked to live, to gather and enjoy friends and family almost every day. It is the opposite in America, where people live to work. This led me to realize that although they missed me, life went on without me. Meanwhile, I was spending my time suffering. For nearly a year and a half, I suffered with colds and headaches. My body was struggling physically to be in two places at once.

My husband always said that enjoying life was the "duty" of a human being. Here I was, physically and emotionally suffering because of a decision I made and did not regret. I started writing everything I felt. Soon I came to realize that I had to end my sorrow and devote myself to live the life I had decided to have and enjoy my new family, which at that time was just me and my husband. I made the decision to stop the suffering by starting to love myself and stop living in the past.

Exercise has always helped me fight depression and sadness, so from the very beginning I looked for a place and found the YWCA of Elgin. There I met Andrea Fiebig, an inspirational woman who I love and respect for her great interest in helping the Latino community by providing English, exercise and health classes. One day the aerobics teacher missed the class. Andrea encouraged me to teach it. The class was a success and that's how my career as a health educator began.

As I worked on recovering my happiness, I remembered that I had always had a dream to be a dancer and an actor. Due to my life circumstances, I could never do it in Mexico, so I started looking for people interested in theater in Spanish and founded the group "Los Desarraigados" (the Uprooted). I chose the children's play "Los Gatos Valerosos", written by my brother, playwright Ignacio Betancourt, to present. I remembered once talking to a professional actor who told me the play would be too difficult to perform with unskilled actors who had to impersonate animals. I decided to direct the play anyway, and we presented the show in different theaters within the local school district. It was a total success! Families got involved and it was a wonderful experience for both the community and me. Behind the curtain, I cried several times from the emotion and joy of having made my dream come true. It confirmed that no matter how old you are or how many negative people block your projects, you should always fight for your dreams.

HAPPINESS IS SHARING THE BICULTURAL

When I analyze my feelings and examine how my self-esteem was once gone, I wonder if other Latinos feel the same way. I remember that while I was at school learning English, I met a lot of people who needed to be heard and recognized as human beings. Almost all of them were living in the past, reminiscing as I had done when I arrived. What struck me was that some of them already had lived many years in the U.S. and were still not feeling part of it. Women and men who left everything to seek a better quality of life in the U.S. were still longing for life in their former villages, among their family and friends. However, they had been called to this country in some way or another and were still also trying to live a life here. Sometimes, they did not even have four hours of sleep because they needed to work two or three jobs to survive.

My journaling in my early years in the U.S. and my experiences helping my husband cope with his illness, all prepared me physically, emotionally and mentally for my work as a mental health educator. I created workshops on self-acceptance, nutrition, and yoga classes that help others. Through these workshops and sessions, people learn to deal with their emotions and overcome fears by loving, respecting and accepting themselves. Here I apply breathing techniques that are very useful in our life, and encourage us to live in the present without thinking about the past or worrying about the future.

I also continue learning and coping with my husband's condition and its causes. He had two more heart attacks and one ended in open-heart surgery. We deal with it on a daily basis, enjoying each day since it is the only thing that we have for sure. It has been a wonderful experience to live with all kinds of people and understand that no matter where we come from or how we're educated, there's a reason why we are in this world. We can live harmoniously by learning to respect and love all living things. If some of us are not good, all of us are not good.

It is ironic that by coming to live in the last country on my list of places to visit I learned to really find me, forgive me, and love me. This led me to have a more harmonious relationship with the beings I love and live with every day.

I am happy now living in the U.S. I have confirmed that one should never judge anything until we live it firsthand. When I'm in Mexico, I enjoy it because I love it and I cannot deny my roots. There always comes a time, though, when I want to return to my current country and see my immediate family, my husband, my two four-legged girls, Camila and Maya, and my chosen extended family and friends, who together make my life complete.

REFLECTION

1. Do you listen to your feelings? What are they telling you? Do you follow or do you try to ignore them?

2. Do you need someone or something else to feel whole? If so, why do you give control of your life away?

3. Inner peace is a reflection of the harmony in your life. How much time do you spend to achieve it?

BIOGRAPHY

Guadalupe "Pita" Betancourt, a physical-emotional mental health educator, was born in San Luis Potosí, México and moved to the U.S. in 1997. Since her youth, Pita has advocated for social justice and equal rights for underserved groups (indigenous, economically disadvantaged women, and Latino immigrants) in Mexico and the U.S. She has worked for DIF Estatal (children and family services), Human Rights Watch, YWCA of Elgin, The Larkin Center, Movimiento Navista and was founder and president of MORENA Illinois (Movimiento de Regeneración Nacional), and founder and director of the theater group "Los Desarraigados". At the YWCA, Pita translated and implemented The Project Active (The Cooper Institute) to promote healthy habits, exercise and food choices as a way of life. At The Larkin Center, she offered counseling and designing workshops on self-esteem and nutrition to the Spanish speaking population.

As a health educator in her business, "Accepting Yourself", she offers personalized yoga instruction for kids, teenagers, adults and seniors, individual and group counseling (featuring her self-esteem and nutrition workshops) and public speaking on nutrition, mental and emotional issues.

Guadalupe "Pita" Betancourt
pita@acceptingyourselfbybetancourt.com
(847) 337-4441

Luisa Fernanda Cicero

"Sometimes the biggest accomplishment in life is to find yourself."

If "home is where the heart is," I'm fortunate that the heart is a powerful muscle.

I was born in Bogotá, Colombia. As a young child, my father relocated to Puerto Ordaz, Venezuela. For the following eight years, I had the best time of my life. In addition to being the birthplace of my brother, I remember Venezuela as the home where I established strong values, life-long friendships, and memories that nourish, inspire and comfort me to this day.

After my dad stopped working in Venezuela, we moved back to Colombia. I realized that every time I moved, my heart was going to split, stretch, and grow. I would need to adapt to new circumstances, which was a particular challenge for me as a teenager at the time.

When I decided to study journalism and social communications, my parents sent me for a few months to Australia to learn English. I embraced another challenge. I travelled to Australia and New Zealand, met great people from all over the world, bungee jumped, scuba dived, created friendships that still exist and started discovering who I was deep inside, away from home.

My love for writing grew stronger and stronger. I began collecting little papers with notes, poems or whatever came to mind. During that time, life changed completely and my family began to fall apart. My parents divorced. In just a few years, everybody left. My mother moved to Australia after she and her fiancée received death threats following the release of his book about the impact of the narcotrafficking on social behavior in Colombia. My dad also moved away, pursuing new employment opportunities in Florida. My brother was a teenager and joined my dad.

There I was, with a fragmented mind, fragmented family and uncertainty about what to do next. At that moment, all I wanted to do was run away, write a new story, find a new and exciting chapter to be part of and leave nothing behind. I felt strong and scared at the same time, but I had nothing to lose. In my mind, I had already lost the most valuable asset in my life: regular contact with my family. Once again, I learned to adapt, to change plans on the fly and be independent. Today I tell my boys, "My job as your mother is to enable you to be independent. You can love me and feel that love, no matter where I am, but you must never depend on that to be the best version of yourself."

180 DEGREES

I remember going to the office of my boss one morning. Joaquín Herrera was a great man and mentor. He listened attentively as I told him I had applied for a scholarship to study antique restoration in Europe. He looked at me with disbelief. "What?" he said, in disbelief. After a long conversation, we had a plan. He would search for opportunities in the company outside of Colombia. I waited, though perhaps impatiently. Three years later, with Joaquin's help, I received a personal offer from the company's headquarters. Four months later, I moved to Naperville, Illinois.

Life changed for me completely. New city. New country. New language. Challenging new job.

I became a workaholic, travelled a lot, achieved and overachieved. Even though everything was new, I remained true to my essence. So I hugged and kissed though it was now culturally inappropriate. I took chances and spoke with my accent. Often, my speech unintentionally sounded like curse words. So I learned to make a disclaimer up front. My cultural quirks became a strength.

As immigrants, I believe the biggest mistake we can make is to blend in so much that we lose our identity. Yes, we always want to be strong and adapt. But we never want to lose our unique soul. People and systems are willing to adapt to us if our performance is strong enough.

In the tough times—such as when my oldest son was born prematurely—I received the flexibility I needed, every time. Why? Because I asked. What is the worst thing someone could say? Even if "no" is the answer, you lose nothing by asking. Mike Bushman, my last boss in corporate and great friend said, "Luisa, I never gave you anything. You earned it."

People who say "you can't" often come from a place of fear that may be based in their own experiences. Those are not your experiences. Only you know your capabilities and your resolve. We should listen and learn, but never allow others to direct our journey.

WHO AM I?

Almost seven years ago, I resigned from my corporate career to become a stay-at-home mom, taking on only work assignments with substantial flexibility. I was blessed to have support from Daniel, my husband. I went into autopilot mode, making decisions, taking risks, and sometimes making mistakes, but most of all, learning, growing, stretching, and searching for me. I was exploring, trying to find "that something" that would make me independent again and allow me to make a difference.

I made the decision to dig deep, to look at my God-given talents, to find something that would allow me to be home with the kids, make a difference, achieve professional fulfillment and develop the woman within. That is when I created the concept of living in my five circles: Spirituality, Family, Career (training, coaching and mentoring), Personal Journey (writing), Making a difference (medical interpreter on missionary trips, non-profit work). From that moment, I decided that everything outside those circles had a simple answer: "No."

Is life perfect? I wish. To deal with difficult challenges, though, I have been blessed with people who provide mutual support from a place of understanding and profound compassion, without judgment.

In my heart, my five circles create a path toward my greater purpose. Sometimes I have to answer questions about my nontraditional choices. Those questions can shake my confidence and threaten my sense of self-worth. In these low points, I remember what I have accomplished. I look at my children and the young men they are becoming. I think about the people who remain in my life and those who have already served a purpose. They have all taught me something and I have given them something too.

Who am I? Someone like you, creating something I can leave as legacy, giving my talent, time and energy to those who need it, taking every day like it may be the last, preserving my inner-self so I can be my best. I strive to make an impact on life and live in a way that I can achieve all the possibilities in my heart.

Home is "where the heart is," but it turns out that "home" for me is everywhere and everyone who contributes to my five circles. My heart is with all of them.

REFLECTION

1. When you look at yourself, do you focus on your gaps or do you fill them with gold, learn from them, and create a better story to tell? What is your story?

2. Are you waiting for something to change or do you believe in creating possibilities? Do you know that YOU are the possibility?

3. How do you embrace your "uniqueness" in a society that celebrates "copy paste" and "let's be like everyone else"? How do you make it your strength?

BIOGRAPHY

Luisa Fernanda is married to Daniel and mother of two smart and compassionate kids: Nicolas and Francesco. She is also CEO of Kintsugi, LLC, an organization focused on bringing out the best in people and organizations through their breaking points and the power of resilience.

As Leadership Development and Communications Coach, Luisa brings over sixteen years of global experience to her clients. She is an author and bilingual public speaker whose leadership trainings have been attended by over 3,000 employees and leaders across Latin America and the Unites States of America.

During her years in Training and Development in her Corporate Career, she co-lead the development of a best-in-class recruiting, hiring and training program in the oilfield industry. She holds a degree in Organizational Communications Management and a B.A in Social Communications and Journalism from "La Universidad de La Sabana," Bogotá, Colombia.

Her passion for writing awakened again a few years ago, when she started writing under the penname: Fermina Ponce. Her first poetry book "AL DESNUDO", was published by Oveja Negra® and launched at the 2016 International Book Fair (FilBo) in Bogotá, Colombia. She currently has another poetry book ready to be published and is working on the outline of her first novel.

Luisa also serves as a medical interpreter during missionary trips supporting "Heart for Honduras." Currently, she also serves on the board for The Fig Factor Foundation, as the Vice President.

Luisa Fernanda Cicero
luisa@kintsugill.com
(630) 999-6130

STUCK . . . OR SUCCESSFUL?
FROM SHOOK-UP TO UNSHAKABLE CONFIDENCE

Jennifer Villarreal

"True success is always moving forward."

If I told you that I'm done chasing success, would you keep reading my story?

It's not true. Actually, I really am done chasing success not because I can't achieve it, but because I've redefined it. When it comes to success, definitions are everything.

In life and in business, we all want to succeed. Like everyone else, I desire to be megasuccessful in everything I do. But I no longer measure success by sales figures, my social calendar, or how many people like my posts.

If you and I are truly going to be successful, we have to ask ourselves, "What does success in my life and business really look like?"

If you are like I once was, your answer might include:

- "If I can just get enough clients to launch my own business, I'll be successful."

- "If I can create a website and business cards that people actually take seriously, I'll be successful."

- "If I can save enough money to quit my day job (finally), I'll be successful."

For thirteen years, this is how I understood success.

The truth was anything but.

MY STORY

If anybody was determined to be successful in business, it was my younger self. As a Latina teenager in a mostly Caucasian school, I never quite fit in with my peers. English is not my first language, but my Spanish also sounds like a five-year-old's, since I forgot most of it as a child. I was introduced to church early and even felt God's presence, but drifted away from Him as I got older.

You might say I was a control freak and prone to depression and suicidal thoughts. My fear and my feisty Latina temperament drove me to do everything on my own, like make my own success. Back then, my definition was simple: "Make lots of money."

I did well enough at first. After college, I bounced through a couple of sales jobs. Each position increased my paycheck, yet somehow it was "never enough". I kept thinking the next opportunity would be my "big break," but my big break seemed perpetually broken. Finally, my never-ending parade of "never enough" collided with the economic downturn of 2007.

Crash!

"Never enough" shattered into "nothing".

While I was picking up the pieces, I decided to become a certified life coach, get coached myself and sell coaching for the biggest names in the industry. Learning how to solve other people's problems did not solve my own, however. I found myself wanting nothing to do with coaching or traditional sales jobs. So I thought perhaps I'd try working in or owning a restaurant like my father had. But that plan soon faded, too. I wound up waiting tables all night, with little more on my plate than a good paycheck and someone else's dinner.

As the years went by, my quest for success brought more stress than I liked to admit. I had no idea what I was meant to do or how to use those gifts in my work. I felt completely stuck.

COPING AND HOPING

To mask the pain and frustration, I tried to fill the void. Drinking, smoking the green stuff, clinging to unhealthy relationships and working overtime became my self-medication for the failure I felt. Even when I had a so-called "success," I still turned to addictive behaviors, because somehow my step forward never quite felt fulfilling.

Take a tip from my experience. Masking pain is not the same as solving it. Nor is it a way to be successful. The opposite of success is being stuck!

When we chase self-worth through money, happiness or possessions, we get stuck. We keep reaching for this thing called "success" but our feet can't step that far.

By this definition, I wasn't just failing. I was knee-deep in quicksand.

At some point, I decided this could not go on. A wise friend suggested sales was "in my DNA," so I switched to a sales job that worked out tolerably well. I put aside my bad habits temporarily and even underwent a process to release the guilt, the shame, resentment, and the things I had done to others and others had done to me. But though I emptied out the negative, I didn't fill back up with anything everlasting.

A few months later, I was back to old habits, feeling more frustrated and angry than ever. Why was success so elusive? Why didn't God seem to care about me at all, if He even existed? In desperation I screamed out to Him to prove He was real.

Four days later, I was hanging out with three friends. My body had had enough of the green stuff, and my knees collapsed. My head hit the floor, and I went into convulsions. I traveled through time and space in ways I can't explain in human terms. In this dark place, I was surrounded by demonic, hooded beings that seemed to tug at me for hours, battling for my soul. (Later, my friends told me it was only a few moments.) I screamed louder than I ever had before. I didn't know I could feel so much pain.

Ultimately, I did survive those terrifying moments, but trust me, you can't stare death in the face and not be affected! For a few days, I tried to convince myself the shaken-up feeling would pass. Yet deep inside, I felt a tug to understand what had happened.

This feeling drew me to visit a woman who recently had cared for my dogs at her amazing retreat facility. I fought the urge to tell her what had happened. As we sat outside, gnats buzzing around us, we drifted through awkward small talk. A lump rose in my throat. I wanted to tell my story, but I felt the way I always had.

Stuck.

Unable to do ... anything.

Finally, I shared my near-death experience in its entirety. My friend and I talked through every block in my heart, including my failed quest for success. Out of that one conversation, I received the best gift ever: renewing my faith in God.

I realized that He had had a purpose for my life all along. What I had chased as "success" was not success at all. It was actually a block that kept me from success. True success is not making money or proving our worth to anyone. It is about always moving forward. Knowing who I now was in Christ, I could develop the unshakable confidence I needed to actually make progress, rather than remaining stuck, masking my fear with addiction and dysfunctional relationships.

I opened my heart to Christ that very afternoon. And that's when the most amazing thing happened. As if from nowhere, a swarm of dragonflies flew in, forty or fifty of them, hovering around me with their shining, rainbow-colored wings! This breathtaking and unexpected event confirmed for me that I had finally found what I was searching for all along.

Once again, I shed all the negative things in my heart. But this time, I not only removed the yucky, I filled up again with all that was unconditionally loving and powerful. I set about serving others rather than chasing dollars. Soon, I sensed an unshakable confidence that released me from my quicksand.

From that moment forward, nothing held me back.

Now I know you're hoping I'll tell you that after this

incredible experience, I made millions of dollars, got booked on a talk show, and moved to Tahiti. That's our old definition of success, remember?

Here's what happened. As I acted on my new understanding about success and my new identity in Jesus, my life ran more smoothly. Instead of feeling angry or anxious when I experienced a challenge, I rested in unconditional love and peace. I developed unshakable confidence that led me to take bolder actions than ever before. I even envisioned launching my new business.

I also reconnected with my Latina heritage and fixed my five-year-old sounding Spanish. As I grew in confidence, I was able to do an hour-long talk in Spanish. I just spoke from my heart without worrying what my audience would think. Plus, I learned that while I may not speak Spanish as well as other Latinas, I sure as heck can out-dance them!

In 2012, I received one of the best gifts ever when I was laid off from my sales job the day after Christmas. This allowed me to fully embrace and launch my business, Sales from the Heart, Inc. Since then, I have been constantly growing. And several times, on the anniversary of my return to God, I've been miraculously visited by dragonflies that re-confirm His guidance. Who could ask for greater success than that?

THE FIVE STAGES OF SUCCESS

My story may sound too beautiful to be true. But all of this did not happen overnight. Just as a dragonfly undergoes different stages of life in order to spread its wings, so we all must undergo five specific stages on our journey into success. This model worked for me and it can work for you, too, in every aspect of life and business.

Stage #1: Clarifying your direction. Ask yourself what you envision for your life and business over the next six to twelve months. For example, have you pushed down a dream or passion from childhood that is trying to resurface? So often, we think we cannot possibly get paid for work we are passionate about! Keep in mind that what you think is possible right now is just what you think is possible. God's vision for your life is much bigger and far-reaching. What might happen if you embraced that vision?

Stage #2: Strategizing your actions. Once you open yourself to an enlarged vision, create an action plan that helps you take steps toward it. Focus on concrete, specific steps that advance your goals.

Stage #3: Upgrading your skills. Once you have determined what steps to take toward your vision, you are ready to list the areas where you would like to improve. Find a class or a mentor to help you work on the areas you identify.

Stage #4: Enhancing your environment. The space in which we work, physically and mentally, has a great effect on us. Seek the support and resources you need to keep a healthy mindset. Search and eliminate those distractions that keep you from being successful.

Stage #5: Mastering the mind-heart shift. Stages 1-4 are critical to success, but without the right beliefs and attitudes in our hearts, we will remain stuck in old patterns, unable to achieve the success we desire. Now is the perfect time to cultivate your redefinition of success. Think powerful thoughts that reaffirm your purpose and vision, and who you are in God's eyes. When your heart and mind are in the right place, you can operate on mission.

REFLECTION

1. How do you personally define success?

2. What beliefs, fears or distractions affect you as you go into your everyday work activities?

3. All perceived barriers aside, where would you like your life and business to be in six to twelve months?

BIOGRAPHY

Jennifer Villarreal has a love for tacos, dogs, and God (and not necessarily in that order)! As a non-traditional sales and marketing catalyst for entrepreneurs who desire more clients and more flexibility, she helps women who feel isolated and stuck to finally move forward with unshakable confidence in life and business. She is the founder of Sales from the Heart, Inc., and the creator of two groundbreaking programs, "Unshakable Confidence" and "Unshakable Identity." Jennifer delivers Spiritual Strength + Heart-based Sales Solutions. She teaches Five Stages of Success to help entrepreneurs truly cast their unique gifts while receiving cash flow from it all. Each 1-to-1 or small group session focuses on implementing action steps that jump-start faith, fun + finances. Her style is warm, direct and always colorful. Humor is non-negotiable! To learn more about Jennifer's LUVgathering™ events, nationwide mentoring, books, audio and video training, or to engage her as a speaker, visit SalesFromTheHeart.com.

Jennifer Villarreal
info@SalesFromTheHeart.com
(773) 614-7253

'FROM RAGS TO RICHES' DOESN'T ALWAYS REFER TO MONETARY WEALTH

Dr. Damary M. Bonilla Rodriguez

"Stay strong as you live your life story and remember your blessings no matter what circumstances you face."

My story is tough to tell because it involves revisiting memories best left in the past. Even so, I tell it on television, radio shows, articles, and online media - in hopes that I can be a positive influence for others.

Born and raised in the underserved, predominantly Hispanic area of New York City known as El Barrio/Spanish Harlem, I am the eldest of three sisters. We lost our mother when I was eight, leaving us in the care of our maternal grandparents with support from extended family, friends, and our church community.

AGAINST ALL ODDS

According to my birth profile, I was supposed to be a negative statistic in the system (foster care, welfare, etc.), with no education or hope of success. My mother became pregnant with me when she was 18 and was pushed to marry my father who was 20 years older than her. Then, my parents separated and my mother moved from New Jersey to New York to be with her family.

My grandmother ended up in a diabetic coma and on the way to see her at the hospital, my mother tripped and fell. From that incident, I was born prematurely. I had some health issues but once ready to go home, my mother took me to live with her and my grandparents. I was named Damary Marcelina, which was my mother's middle name (Edith Damary) and my grandmother's first name. Perhaps my name set me up to be a leader since both matriarchs were tough women who cared about others and made a difference in everyone's lives.

Mom worked hard to take care of me and have an income. When I was two, she began a relationship with her boss. They had a daughter, Carmen, and began a life together in New York. I was left to be raised by my grandparents but never knew why. Blessed to have my mother in my life and so much love around me, I didn't realize that my father was not part of my life; I was a happy child.

Years later, my biological father came to New York to find my mother and they got back together. They moved to Connecticut and had my youngest sister, Erica. I stayed with my grandparents who moved to Connecticut so I could be around my parents and sisters. Later, legal issues pushed my parents to move. When they ended up in Indiana, my grandparents and I moved back to my birth state of New York. The legal issues caught up to my father who was arrested in Indiana and imprisoned for several years at which point, my mother officially became a single mother, raising a child on her own for the first time.

Even though two of her daughters did not live with her, mom regularly spent time with us by picking us up or visiting. Growing up, my sisters and I heard stories about our mother's struggle with unstable finances, relationship issues, domestic violence at the hands of men she loved, and imperfect family dynamics. My mother lived a short but tough life which is probably why I remember every day that we were with her as amazing. What I remember most about my mother is her beautiful smile, how much fun we had when she brought us together, how she respected her parents, and how complete my life was amidst all the chaos in her life.

TRAGEDY CHANGES EVERYTHING

Friday, Jul. 24, 1987 is a vivid reminder for me because that is the day my mother died. We lived in New York and were having dinner on the front steps of our building when one of my aunts came by crying inconsolably. She brought the dreadful news that my mother had been shot and killed. I still remember not understanding because I had never experienced loss before. My grandparents and several family members immediately drove to Connecticut. When we got to the hospital, my mother's death was confirmed; she was just 27 years old. It has been 29 years since her tragic passing and I still cry every time I share my mother's story. Since that sad summer day, I have had to cope with loss too many times. Her death taught me that life is hard and uncertain. Soon after she died, my father was released from prison so my grandparents ended up in New York and New Jersey courts, battling him for custody of me and my youngest sister, Erica. After much heartache, they won and we hoped to live a somewhat normal life.

Loss means someone leaves you physically, but they never leave your heart or memories. Once you say goodbye, you are left to pick up the pieces. For me, that meant my adolescence was full of obstacles. My sister, Erica, and I were being raised by grandparents rather than parents so we had to handle adult responsibilities from a young age and grew up in a low-income housing project in the ghetto.

Since losing my mother, life has been tough but I feel so blessed when I wake up each day. We can allow experiences to knock us down or to be the foundation for a wonderful life. When I reflect on how I made it this far, I credit several key factors: 1) amazing people in my life; 2) a solid spiritual foundation; 3) a strong dose of my Latino culture; and 4) formal and informal education.

I am not rich with money but with love, joy, and fruitful relationships that challenge me and help me grow. Fulfillment derives from: 1) being touched by loved ones who overcome obstacles; 2) interacting with amazing educators and bosses who pique my curiosity for learning; 3) the examples of great leaders whose lives resonate with mine; 4) pride in being a Latina leader in the U.S.; and 5) faithfulness to the spiritual foundation that I have known from childhood.

STANDING STRONG ON MY FOUNDATION

As a child, I prayed to God and still pray every day. I have also taught my boys about prayer knowing it will help them through life. I believe one finds peace through a solid relationship with God or another deity. My relationship with God carried me through a tough childhood of poverty and challenges, the loss of several important loved ones, and the journey to accessing higher education while working and raising a younger sibling. I also know that my spiritual beliefs helped me overcome sexual abuse, teenage eating disorders, and health issues including anxiety and difficulty conceiving.

This chapter shares the parts of my story that aren't public. Trying to find a balance in my chaotic life pushed me to bulimia and anorexia. Pushing through the eating disorders and sorting through life led to anxiety disorder. As a teen and in college, I saw therapists and leaned on my faith to help me deal with my issues. Seeking help allowed me to realize that some things were out of my control, but I could still control how I was, or was not affected. Acceptance came slowly and missing my loved ones shifted to fondly remembering them, knowing that they're always with me. Renewed faith allowed me to push ahead in life no matter what I faced.

In high school, I was an active community volunteer and held leadership roles at church and school, while working after school. I went straight to college and resided in a dorm. The transition was hard for my grandmother because she did not want to let me go; she regularly made my grandfather drive 40 minutes to see me. After my first year in college, I moved in with my high school sweetheart, Robert. A few months later, we took custody of my youngest sister. She was fourteen and we were nineteen.

In hindsight, the first decade that Robert and I lived together was life practice because after that we got married, built a house, and had babies. We have been in a relationship for nineteen years without a break so we have grown into adulthood together with intense support of one another. He is my number one fan and has always encouraged me to pursue my dreams. I completed a B.A. in Spanish and Social Work where I graduated with Departmental Honors, made the Dean's List on several occasions, earned the College President's Medal, and was awarded Sigma Delta Pi. Education has been my key to dealing with stress so I continued my educational journey until I earned an M.S. in Organizational Communications and a Specialized Certification in Corporate Communications.

I also earned my highest degree - Doctor of Education with a focus in Executive Leadership - while working and being pregnant with twins. My research, A Profile of Latina Leadership in the United States: Characteristics, Positive Influences, and Barriers (Bonilla-Rodriguez, 2011), has been referenced at conferences and in speeches, as well as used for program/ curriculum development and professional trainings across the U.S. I have worked toward the leadership development of youth, women, and the Latino community through active community service and mentorship.

My greatest accomplishment, though, is raising my six-year-old twins, Joshua Marc and Caleb Isaiah. Robert and I were told that we would never have biological children but with prayer and medical assistance, we received a double blessing. Their names were chosen from the Bible and we are raising them to be God-fearing men who will be productive members of society and uphold their family's legacy of perseverance.

My family has experienced terminal illness, long term incarceration, autism, cerebral palsy, genetic diseases, domestic violence, and tragedy at its worst but we stand strong on the values and principles taught to us. I am grateful to have had the privilege to care for my grandparents until they passed, just as they cared for my sisters and me. The result of their love and commitment is that they raised hardworking women. My sisters make me proud every day and I know that our mom and grandparents watch proudly from above. Carmen is a Licensed Master Social Worker (LMSW) and strong advocate for autism awareness. Erica is a police officer with a B.A. in Criminal Justice. We all have wonderful husbands, beautiful children, and own our own homes.

While my path has been difficult, I pride myself in being a Latina who is determined to fight for others and improve society. I thank God, my grandparents, and others who carried me against all odds. My life story is still being written but my journey from the projects in the ghetto of New York City, to a custom-built house in a gated community in the Poconos is one that took me from being a poor orphan, to being a "rich" woman in ways not related to money.

I am a strong believer of what the Bible says in Luke 12:48: "To whom much is given, much will be required." There is still work for me to do and more to give. The moral of my story is that the impossible can become possible, if you set your mind to it. My tips for success in navigating life's circumstances are to: 1) stay close to your loved ones, 2) go after your goals, 3) keep your head up through life's trials, 4) don't doubt yourself, and 5) be sure to lift others up. Finally, remember my quote: "stay strong and remember your blessings no matter what circumstances you face."

REFLECTION

1. Reflect on your biggest losses. How have/can you overcome loss and made/make it a positive aspect of your life experience?

2. Do you have a spiritual foundation to help you stay grounded in tough times? If not, is this something that can help you find peace and get grounded in life?

3. What unfinished business do you have in life? How can you accomplish these goals?

BIOGRAPHY

Dr. Damary M. Bonilla-Rodriguez is a nationally known, leading authority on leadership development as it pertains to diversity and inclusion. Her research on Latina leadership in the U.S. has inspired events, conference sessions, publications, and content development to address the urgency of creating a pipeline of diverse leaders within this fast-growing population.

She holds a B.A. in Spanish and Social Work, an M.S. in Organizational Communication, and a Specialized Certification in Corporate Communications, all from the College of New Rochelle. She earned a Doctorate in Education focusing on Executive Leadership from St. John Fisher College.

She received a proclamation from the NYS Assembly and was selected as a 2014 Coors Light "Lideres" finalist and is a contributor to the Huffington Post. Her work around leadership and empowerment of women has been featured on NBC Latino's "Latina Leaders" series, Chief Writing Wolf, and Proud to be Latina's "Empowered Latinas" series. She is a board member of Latina VIDA, Latinas on the Plaza, and Los Compadres Modern Caballero, as well as an advisor to the Board of Hispanic Caucus Chairs and the Alliance for Positive Youth Development, among others.

Dr. Damary M. Bonilla-Rodriguez
alatinaleadershipprofile@gmail.com
(646) 269-2692

Jennifer Vera

"The moments that define us, and test us to our core,
are blessings in disguise."

I was in yoga class when it hit me. I had just been through a difficult breakup that had destroyed me. Hanging in downward dog, I realized I was deeply unhappy with every single aspect of my life – not just the breakup part. On the outside, it didn't seem like I had much to be sad about. I had a good job, was very involved with my community and had tons of friends. Yet here I was in a class of 15 strangers on my mat, weeping my eyes out. What was wrong with me?

My journey into entrepreneurship isn't like most because I didn't exactly plan it. What I did plan was a five-month journey halfway across the world to India, Myanmar, Indonesia, and Europe (my so-called *Eat Pray Love* trip). I had big plans for this trip. I would find peace and happiness (and maybe a husband) and then I would come back home victorious and wise. I had my trip mapped out on an Excel spreadsheet with the festivals I'd attend, where I would stay, and when I would get there. I had even accepted a position upon my return, one that was willing to wait six months for me to start.

My life was set, or so I thought.

THE UNPLANNED

"I want to show you the real Rishikesh, not just the touristy part. Come with me on my motorcycle. I promise I will get you back to your ashram by curfew," said Hemu, an Indian guide I had met that afternoon.

I had just spent a month and half backpacking through the south of India and found myself at the foothills of the Himalayas up north in a small yoga town called Rishikesh. I'd done a 10-day meditation, stayed at an ashram with an awakened teacher and of course, crossed so many things off of my famous Excel document. The "real" Rishikesh was packed full with people wandering the streets. Markets and streetlights from the evening rush. "You can buy things here at a fraction of what they charge where you're staying," Hemu informed me. I wasn't in the mood for shopping and the mountain air was cold at night. I had worn an Indian-style outfit I had bought in the south of India which consisted of very thin material. It was fine for Rishikesh during the day, where the temperatures got up to 80 degrees, but at 50 degrees now, and on a motorcycle riding fast, I found it lacking. Freezing, I felt so alive riding up and down the mountains of this sacred city.

Hemu took me through a nature reserve with roads seldom used at night because of the wild elephants. We stopped at a vista point there, despite my protest because of the cold. We walked up this tall rock until we could see to the other side. In the mountains and overlooking Rishikesh, I took in the beauty of the small town lit up at night with its long bridges overlooking Mother Ganga. The view was worth the cold.

I started down the rock. It was dark, and that's when it happened.

I must have screamed because before I knew it, Hemu was there and he was freaking out. I looked at my leg and saw the bone, white and broken, through my skin. "Oh shit."

"Hemu, you need to go down to Rishikesh and you need to bring an ambulance back here," I said more calmly than I would have ever expected to be under the circumstances.

"You don't understand, this is India – it's not America! How am I going to find an ambulance? The nearest hospital is far away; can you get on the motorcycle?" His phone had no reception in the mountains. My only chance was for him to bring help back to me and given his hysterical condition, I wasn't sure what the chances of that were, but I had no choice.

"My bone is sticking out of my body, I cannot get on your motorcycle. Find help! Go, now!" I responded.

With his hands over his mouth in shock he got on his motorcycle and I was left alone on the Himalayan mountainside. I was uncertain as to whether I would see Hemu again. He was quite hysterical and in the time we'd been along this road I hadn't seen or heard another car pass by. I was enveloped by a silence only broken by my screams. "Help me! Somebody please help me!" I had never known my own voice until that night – the shrill sound, the desperation and the sheer volume of it. Not one headlight shone; not one hint of anyone listening to my cries. The white of my bone was sticking out of my bloody shin. The night was silent and unresponsive to my calls and I was alone. It was at that moment that I remembered the reason cars didn't drive down this road at night: wild elephants.

So I prayed. I grabbed the mala beads around my neck that the awakened teacher had blessed and started chanting the mantra she had gifted me. It was all I could do to not pass out from the pain. At that moment, I realized something so profound within my soul and within my body that I never really understood until that moment. You can call it God, you can call it surrender but to me it will always be wordless, formless and limitless. It was the idea that I have no control. This notion of control I had with all my fancy travel plans and intense Excel sheets listing my itineraries and sights to see, my imagined trajectory for my life, marriage, children, and jobs rendered meaningless in one moment. It's all an illusion.

Four hours I was alone there on that mountainside, staring at the night sky, chanting between my cries and then soothed by surrender, remaining present with my breath. The word "relief" cannot even describe how I felt the moment I saw a white, square truck on the empty road. The ambulance had arrived.

THE FAILED PLAN

Seventeen excruciating days in the hospital in India landed me with a titanium rod in my tibia. I had broken both bones and was immobile. Plans for Myanmar, Indonesia and Europe were scrapped and I returned home to the polar vortex of Chicago on crutches. Less than two months after my less than stellar return home, my grandfather passed away.

Memories of my extended summer stays in his bungalow on Chicago's south side flooded my mind. I remembered holding his hand as a little girl going to the panadería, or later hanging out with him drinking tea and talking about his life in Mexico, or the latter part of his life massaging his swollen legs. Grief filled my heart as I gimped around my house, still not fully mobile. The only thing I was looking forward to doing was starting my new job, a fresh start in a new field, something I could pour myself into.

Before my spiritual adventures, I was obsessed with my career. I had always been pretty ambitious, I loved to serve and as such wound up in the nonprofit world of economic development. I founded a young professionals board for the Hispanic Alliance for Career Enhancement (HACE) and served on various other boards from the American Heart Association to the Chicago Community Trust. Typical to my Type A personality, I loved working and more than that, running things. I wasn't one to sit still, yet here I was – with nothing but forced stillness and time.

The moment finally came for me to start my new position. I sat in the chair of the office waiting for the CEO. He came in the room, overly warm and friendly, and we made our small talk. "Jen, I'm sorry, we lost a lot of money on this deal. We can't bring you in at this time." All my hopes had been pinned on starting fresh, on putting the roughness and emotional and physical pain behind me through this job. It was that same suit of armor I used before my trip to India – keep so busy with work that you can't see how incredibly unhappy you are. I'd have no out this time. I looked at his eyes, numb and detached. "Okay," I said, and stepped out into the cold Chicago evening air.

This was the defining moment. There was nothing anyone could say to me. Nothing anyone could do to me. I realized in that moment I was now immune from disappointment and it was then that I was ready.

THE NEW PLAN

"Kristin, I need a logo," I said to my childhood best friend who was visiting from Mexico City. I put the finishing touches on my website and posted all over my social media that I was now a business (one that had no idea what it was they did exactly), but no matter – I was for hire! Shortly thereafter, I had a new client mention she loved my website. "Want one?" I didn't wait to figure out exactly what I was doing (not something I recommend). I just took action. After so much of shedding identities in the six months prior, I knew two things: 1) I had a very defined purpose in this world to empower others into their purpose and 2) I was an entrepreneur – my soul was an entrepreneur.

For me, being such an experiential learner, I had to go through an intense string of events for me to understand who I really was. I had to realize there was no grand plan – only this emptiness and the immense power of a moment. After all, emptiness' greatest grace is that there's only space to create, and I was a creator.

My soul was rocked to its core in such a way that I had no choice but to shed the identities I had poured over myself to hide from what I really was. When I set out on my adventure to India, my intent was to have a spiritual journey. Truthfully, what happened is that the journey didn't begin until I landed back home. Then that journey permeated every aspect of my life, especially my journey into entrepreneurship.

That same self-seeking into my own core was exactly what guided me to create my company, Vera Strategies. Vera Strategies helps align purpose and passion into an integrous brand and launch it out into the world. In short, I help others do what I did – unhide from who they really are by building a strong brand that will attract their ideal clients. Since founding the company in October of 2014, I've moved to Miami and co-founded a collective called The Creative Girls, where my partners and I help women entrepreneurs position their brands, create authentic brand visuals and find and nurture their tribe through social media.

The moments that define us and test our core, are blessings in disguise. In the end, I learned that no matter what happens to me – if I fail at something, if I go through another one of those bad break-ups or if I'm rejected by a big client or God forbid, have another accident, there is a part of me that will ALWAYS be okay. My core being knows this and understands that it's all part of the journey and there are no Excel sheets that can predict the ride.

REFLECTION

1. What do you do when your plans go astray? What should you do?

2. Have you ever experienced a time of forced inactivity? What did you learn from it?

3. Is your immersion in work or other activities keeping you from expressing your authentic identity? What can you do to bring it out into the world?

BIOGRAPHY

Jennifer Vera creates compelling digital brand identities and unique brand positioning for creators, thought leaders and impact entrepreneurs. She is founder of Vera Strategies, a digital brand and web development company and cofounder/partner of The Creative Girls, a collective of branding experts in Miami.

She is known as an innovative, strategic and energetic creative. Her unique blend of business strategy, brand positioning and creativity activate clients to step into their vision with clarity, direction and passion.

Jennifer does what she does because she believes there "must be a stronger counter culture to Kardashian culture". Prior to founding Vera Strategies, Jennifer spent a decade developing a diverse set of skills working hands on with entrepreneurs and nonprofit organizations in leadership, communication and strategy in her hometown of Chicago. Learn more about Jennifer @ verastrategies.com or @thecreativegirls.com.

Jennifer Vera
jennifer@verastrategies.com
(847) 630-5619

Teresita Marsal-Avila

"Only you can define your future."

My mother is an extremely independent force of nature who always knew what she wanted and how to get it. Her attitude has guided me from Communist Cuba to her family's dream homeland…the U.S.

Recently, I stood in front of the Latino Law Student Association at my alma mater to receive an alumni award and I looked out in amazement. In the 1980's, I was the sole member of the organization. I met with Professor Moskowitz regularly and would ask him "Why are we doing this?" He basically explained as in the film, Field of Dreams, "if you build it, they will come." I waited three years for another Latino to attend the Law School. Now the minority population at Valparaiso is up to 48 percent. Like me, they are all determined to achieve their dream. For me, that meant life in three different countries with radically different governments, and my mother's persistence guiding us through them all.

LIFE IN CUBA

I was born in Cuba in 1960, a year after the Castro regime

rose to power. Seemingly overnight, the country changed. Soon, the only way to do things was the government's way. Old history books disappeared. Churches closed. Lining up for food rations became the norm. "Watchdogs" moved into the neighborhood to report suspicious activity. We learned the communist manifesto. It would have been all I ever knew, if it were not for my parents.

Our middle class home was secretly against the regime. We were a democracy with my strong, determined mother as the dictator. She was deeply religious and a stalwart believer in education. "Things can come and go," she used to say, "but what you learn…nobody can ever take that away from you." My parents had married in a church, but could now be arrested for having a bible or teaching me and my younger brother Alberto anything about their faith. My father, who worked with IBM systems at the electric company, was forced into military service on night watch in case the "Yankees" came. Secretly, he hoped they would so he could surrender!

My lessons at home were a sharp contrast to lessons at school. School taught that Americans were imperialist, destructive enemies. At home, my parents said America would rescue the country. They also taught me about God, so when some men came into the classroom with lovely snacks and asked if the food came from God or Fidel, I was very confused when only those children who chanted "Fidel," "Fidel," Fidel," enjoyed the snacks.

At school, I was a model student but not part of the Cuban Pioneers, a scout-like organization. One time, we were asked to write an essay praising the government and mine was selected as the best. Without telling my mother or me ahead of time, they dressed me as a Cuban Pioneer and took me in a bus to a meeting where I had to read my essay to a very large crowd of people. The hypocrisy and manipulation fell heavily on my mother's heart.

My parents were hatching a plan to get to America by first fleeing to Spain, which was accepting refugees. It was devastating for my mother to think of leaving my grandmother, but she put her children first. She was determined that her children should have a proper education, faith, and freedom.

We finally found a legal way to leave but it involved money—and not Cuban pesos, but American dollars. My uncle, who already lived in the U.S., saved for us and helped us get what we needed. However, since everything we had-- from the house we lived in to the clothes on our back as well as our free education-- technically belonged to the government, we had to "pay them back" before we could leave the country. They took an inventory of everything in the house and told us to have everything there on the day we left. Then they took my father away to a labor camp to pick tomatoes and cut sugar cane for the government without pay for nearly three years. He had always had a desk job so the physical strain of the hard labor often made him ill. Meanwhile, my mother had an underground job taking care of an older lady and carefully avoided the "watchdogs". At the age of eight, I was given the responsibility of cooking, cleaning and taking care of my brother. I watched in amazement as she worked tirelessly to keep our family moving towards freedom.

ON TO SPAIN

It was August of 1971 when without warning, we received a telegram that it was time to leave. My mother threw a few things into a bedsheet and before we knew it, we were out of our home and stripped of our possessions, our dignity, and our humanity. The airport was terrifying. We were hounded about paperwork and VISAS by intimidating military men with cocked weapons ready to fire. I will never forget boarding the airplane. While my terrified parents shook in fear, I heard Cuban military soldiers yell at us, "Do not look back, or you will never leave this country. You are traitors to the Revolution and you will never be allowed back in." We noticed the plane that we boarded was Cuban instead of Spanish and we wondered if we were being flown to our death. But our extreme fear turned to extreme relief when our plane finally touched down in Madrid.

Spain had a program for refugees and gave us a card for medical care and food. The country was a dictatorship, and we were now poor and without relatives, but Spain felt like heaven to us. Here we could freely speak, think and pray. Nobody was watching or following us. The most important thing was finding a job. My mother eventually became a maid in a house of nobility where she was treated well and my dad found a data entry job.

My mother has always been a fighter, with faith as her armor. When she was told that there was no room in the public school for me, she marched into a private, Catholic school and enrolled me. To this day I don't know how I got into such an expensive, upper class school. But I was getting educated, just as she wanted.

We only lived in Spain for two years, but I will always be grateful for the country's welcoming arms. In 1973, with the help of my uncle and a Catholic Charities refugee program, we boarded a plane for America…our final destination!

HARD WORK IN AMERICA

We settled in with my uncle in a New Jersey town which was an easy commute to Manhattan. My parents found factory work, but my mother prayed feverishly for something more suitable for my father. One day she heard of a fellow Cuban who was working at Chase Manhattan bank in Manhattan. He was able to get my father an interview for a position in data processing.

The day of the interview, my mother took us all to the train station with my father. He didn't want to go. He didn't even know English, yet the family's future was riding on this interview. My mother pulled him close by his coat lapels, as if transferring all her strength and determination to him. "You have to do this!" she said, for she always believed we defined our own future. "Nothing is impossible if you make up your mind to do it," she would always say. My father got the job at the bank branch in lower Manhattan and worked there for 20 years before retiring. He spent many lunch hours in the cafeteria which faced the Statue of Liberty, an eternal icon for his freedom and new homeland.

For me, America was strange and difficult. At school, I didn't know the language so I was placed in a remedial, unruly and disruptive seventh grade class. On the first day of school, I had to share a locker with a girl. "Be sure to be back at 3:00 to get your stuff because my mom is picking me up," she said. However, at 3:00, when I tried to leave, the teacher yelled at me in English. I didn't know that my unruly class ALWAYS stayed after school. Needless to say, I missed getting my things out of the locker. I ended up lost and walking home in the cold, dark January night, and finally arrived three hours late. For the first time ever, I told my mother I didn't want to go to school anymore. Can you imagine her reaction? I was back the next day.

In junior high, I exceled in math because it didn't require much English. High school, however, was much better. With English mastered, I was now able to perform well in all my classes. I was a perfectionist and would settle for nothing less than 100 percent. My mother always told me our legacy would be our education and work ethic. I easily moved to the head of the class. Shy and foreign, I was very different from the other "smart" kids in my honors classes that had grown up together. I was the outsider, who wrecked the class curve by getting 100 percent on tests, so they alienated me. They taught me that if I wanted to succeed, I needed to do it on my own.

Today I work as an immigration lawyer, but my first impression of a courtroom was from the TV show, "Perry Mason". My father explained how there were no fair courtrooms in Cuba and lawyers needed to defend the rights of others. I decided that was what I wanted to do, but when I consulted my high school guidance counselor, she flatly discouraged me. "You have two strikes against you," she said. "First, you're a woman. And second, you're a Latina." She asked me if I wanted to be something else like a social worker or a teacher. I thanked her politely and left the room. I had already defined my future. I was going to be a lawyer. And if I had to do it on my own, against all odds, I would.

Money was the deciding factor for my college choice, and the largest scholarship—a full ride—came from Valparaiso University in Indiana. It was the best decision of my life. Even though there were few Latinos there, the people were nice, open-minded, and had similar values. I received my law degree there too, and after working with a firm for several years, I opened my own immigration law practice in the "Little Village" area of Chicago. In 2013, I added a second location in the western suburb of Oak Brook. I can easily relate to fellow Latinos and immigrants who are desperately trying to assimilate to the U.S. I also understand the pain of not being able to return to the loved ones left behind in your homeland.

Today, I am happily married to a man who understands my values and work ethic. Our daughter, Melissa, also has a fervor for justice and has chosen law as her profession. My father died in 2013, never having returned to Cuba and still dreaming that his beloved homeland would someday be free. My mother lives with me. She continues to be my inspiration as she has fought a winning battle against cancer for the past 20 years. Her strength, sacrifices and unyielding faith are my legacy.

Looking back, I have found that those "two strikes" that my guidance counselor mentioned were actually assets. They helped me define my future against the odds, and have made me the strong lawyer, entrepreneur and capable woman I was meant to be.

BIOGRAPHY

Teresita Marsal-Avila's path to becoming one of Chicago's most recognized and respected immigration advocates has been a long and interesting one. Born and raised in Cuba, Teresita and her family fled the Castro regime to live as refugees in Spain. She arrived in the U.S. as an adolescent, bringing with her only the constant refrain of the lesson taught to her by her mother - that though every material possession might be taken, an education was yours forever. Teresita dedicated herself to her studies and graduated at the top of her high school class. She was awarded a full scholarship to attend Valparaiso University where she earned her B.A. in History in 1983 and her J.D. (Juris Doctor) in 1986. In 2005, Teresita opened the doors of her own legal practice in Chicago's Little Village and offers both legal counsel and employment opportunities. In October of 2013, she added a location in Oak Brook, IL. Teresita has lived several lives: child raised in a repressive government, refugee, immigrant, legal professional, entrepreneur, wife, mother, and daughter. She has learned that circumstances can be changed, the human spirit soars when confronted with obstacles, God and family come first

 and that paying it forward is an obligation we all share.

Teresita Marsal-Avila
teresita@tma-law.com
(773) 762-2500

Fanny Mairena

"Face challenges, fear, and frustration by seeking out knowledge and opportunities for growth."

Challenges occur in all stages of life. How you deal with these challenges directly impacts your ability to grow, improve, and achieve your goals. As a strong Latina woman, I have learned these lessons over and over. And, I expect to continue to learn such lessons for the rest of my life.

Like many children, my early childhood began happily and was filled with love. However, one day uncertainty became a large part of my life when my mother, a loving, wonderful mom and teacher, decided to move to New York City, leaving me behind in the Dominican Republic to be raised by my grandmother and aunt. Despite the best intentions of my aunt and grandmother, I became shy and insecure. Of course, they loved me and did an exceptional job of raising me, but I longed for my mother.

I was also missing my father, a politician in the province of Bahoruco in the Dominican Republic. He was well respected and beloved by his community, enough so that he held office for three terms. He was very busy with his career. Also, his relationship with my mother had ended badly and my family disapproved of my desire to have a relationship with my father. I often felt empty, as if a piece of me was missing.

The absence of both my parents was one of the earliest challenges I had to face in my life. The more I missed them, the more I began to focus on my education in order to cope. This set the stage for many triumphs throughout my life whenever I faced challenges and struggle. Through my studies, I began to develop courage to try new things. My eyes were opened to other possibilities for my future, and I began to dream of a brighter, bolder life for myself. I also developed a sense of optimism that prepared me for the next chapter — New York City.

A NEW CITY, LANGUAGE AND WAY OF LIFE

When I was 12, I suddenly found myself reunited with my mother. She was no longer a teacher, but instead had become a home health aide, working with and supporting children with HIV and AIDS in New York City. The work was not glamorous, but my mother consistently and constantly worked hard in order to support me. She even arranged for me to follow her to the U.S. and instilled the importance of education in me. But what was a young girl, not yet a teenager, supposed to do in a new city with a language she didn't speak?

Imagine the shock of arriving in a huge city after growing up on a small island. Imagine your first view of the city at night, rising up in the midst of the dark. There were the bright lights of New York, something I had only seen in pictures until then. I wish it had been a moment of excitement and joy, but in truth, I was scared. I felt a dark cloud growing within me and felt fear surging through my heart. Was I ready for such a big change?

MY SAVIOR—EDUCATION

Again, I turned to education, but it wasn't as easy as it had been in the Dominican Republic. I was thrown into the public school where English was the norm. I was filled with uncertainty and experienced daily frustrations because of my inability to communicate. It was bad enough being the new kid, but I was also foreign and didn't know the language, the customs, or the expectations. I was bullied, harassed, and made to feel like an outsider over and over. The breaking point was being surrounded by a mob of other female students, poked and prodded, yelled at, and bullied. They were ready to fight and I couldn't understand why.

I decided to fight back by learning. I learned to speak English. I learned to ask for help. I learned to thrive in difficult circumstances. With my limited speaking skills, I shyly approached my teachers and school counselors for help. Little by little, I learned English. I watched, I listened, and applied my new skills consistently and diligently. I read English books, watched English television, and even practiced English at home despite Spanish being the preferred language there. I sought out mentors who complimented my drive to study and learn. I wasn't just open to it — I was hungry for knowledge.

Fast forward six months — no more fights, no more bullying, no more harassment because I couldn't communicate. I was no longer afraid to speak and express myself in English. The better I spoke, the more effectively I studied. The more effectively I studied, the better I did. That shy, insecure little girl from the Dominican Republic had become a confident, smart, motivated young woman.

I went from being the immigrant, Spanish-speaking daughter of a home health aide to a bilingual high school graduate and college freshman.

NEW CHALLENGES AND TESTS OF STRENGTH

When I left the comforts of home in Washington Heights, Manhattan for the campus of State University of New York at Old Westbury in Long Island, I felt like I was reliving my move to New York City. I was filled with uncertainty and fear, but I was also proud of my hard work and efforts that got me there.

At first, I found myself again fearful, worried, and feeling lost and like I didn't belong. I let my confidence fall and small challenges began to feel huge. That's when someone placed a tennis racquet in my hands. I joined the tennis team and my stress and worries began to fall away. With every swing and every ball I hit, I was able to smash fear and conquer worry. I developed a safe haven and a place to banish my negative emotions. Tennis became more than a hobby and more than just a sport to me. It became my comfort, my stress relief, my joy. If I wasn't studying, I was playing tennis, eventually rising in the ranks to be twice nominated Most Valuable Player. Perseverance carried me through turmoil to triumph.

In my first two years of college, tennis helped me create routines and develop habits that eventually helped me choose and succeed in my major. By applying the determination and focus I used in tennis to my classes, I was easily able to learn computer science. I was able to sail past the fact that the subject was male-dominated and immerse myself in learning. I spent so much time in the computer lab that I not only learned programming and other computer skills, but I also started to help others.

Education helped me as a young child in the Dominican Republic, a teenager in Washington Heights in New York City, and a college student in Long Island. With the support of mentors and coaches, I completed my degree in Computer Science with a concentration in Management Information Systems. Me — that little scared girl from the Dominican Republic who used to want nothing more than her parents. I had achieved a huge milestone in life by immersing myself in knowledge.

THRIVING DESPITE TRAGEDY AND INQUALITY

I was on the brink of the next chapter in my life when tragedy struck. It wasn't only my tragedy, but the tragedy of my adopted nation, the United States. As I was preparing myself to enter the work force, everything changed in my beloved New York City. Two commercial airplanes struck two iconic buildings in the heart of the city. It was 9/11 and terrorists had just attacked America. Old feelings of fear returned and with them, came anger. At a time when I should have been excitedly starting my first professional job, I found no available jobs. The city was trying to rebuild, but trust was low and as a result, few companies were hiring. I took whatever jobs were available, hoping and praying for the right opportunity to arrive. I was ready to get on with my life!

As the city and the nation began to recover, my thirst for knowledge was reignited. I was hungry for any opportunity to learn and grow. Unfortunately, my chosen field of computers, engineering, and technology was overrun with men and inequality was everywhere. In fact, gender inequality was so strong in my field that I sometimes wondered if I would ever find a job. I networked with family and friends. I spent countless hours scouring the internet for leads.

As I looked back at everything I had already accomplished, I decided nothing was going to stop me from pursuing my dreams. I had overcome bigger challenges already! My brother suggested a training course, and I enrolled, despite the inconvenient commute. Then, one day I was invited by a Technology Company to interview at the Sun Microsystems New York City office, and I was hired on the spot! I thrived in this job and learned so much, yet I wasn't ready to stop there.

CHOOSING SUCCESS

I grew, learned and did well at the job, but it was not my last stop. I still had so much to learn and accomplish (and I know I still do in the future). I was ready for more challenges. Being both female and a Latina in a male -dominated field was not going to stop me from moving on and building more successes for myself. I learned early on in life that it is an asset to be open to learning, asking for help, and seeking knowledge. I am not afraid to take on new tasks at work or in life, and I am not afraid to make mistakes along the way — in fact, mistakes are opportunities to learn more!

Seeking out opportunities and learning from my mistakes has brought me great rewards. I have embraced a world of learning opportunities that have helped me move out of my comfort zone. I still apply these concepts to my life today and they have never failed. Being curious and open to the world, and willing to work hard for what I believe in, even when all odds are against me, has brought me success, time and time again. This has allowed me to live a fulfilling life and to feel exhilarated by my accomplishments.

Today, I am a system support engineer and the only female and Latina in a group of twenty-two men. I have earned multiple certifications within my field and due to my dedication and hard work, I now have a new role — trainer and mentor.

Throughout my life, I have faced challenges, fear, and frustration by seeking out knowledge and opportunities for growth. When upset with my situation or a problem, I can dwell in my misery and negative feelings or I can get up, brush myself off, and do something to change my situation. I choose the latter.

My message for other young women, and particularly young Latina women, is that your situation today or yesterday does not have to be your situation tomorrow. Challenges are an opportunity to make choices for your future. Will you lay down and let the challenge roll over you or will you stand up and push back, seeking out opportunities for growth and improvement? I have seen so many young girls without motivation and with no desire to move forward. Instead, they choose unhappiness, to stay stuck in negative situations. You can choose success. You can keep looking forward, and keep reaching for your goals. It will be worth it in the long run. You can be smart, successful, and Latina all at the same time.

REFLECTION

1. How do you choose success?

2. How do you view education in your life? Why?

3. What are the opportunities for growth that you face in your life today? What will you do with them?

BIOGRAPHY

Fanny Mairena is Latina woman living and working in New York City as a successful systems support engineer. She has been able to climb the ranks of a male-dominated field by applying lessons of persistence, knowledge-seeking, and self-reliance learned from an early age as a child in the Dominican Republic.

Her childhood ambition, besides obtaining a college degree and building a professional technology career, was to become a business owner. Today, her entrepreneurial spirit has expanded her interests through e-commerce and social media management. She is a passionate advocate for the Latina community. She enjoys lifting up and mentoring young Latina women in New York through her organization, Latinas en New York (LENY).

Her successful life journey is constantly evolving to provide innovative opportunities for Latina women. As a minority and a woman (twice blessed!) she faced many challenges--or, better still, opportunities—as she engaged her vision at every opportunity she was presented with. The success that came her way motivated her even more. She is an amazing mother of three wonderful children and in her spare time, Fanny still loves to smack a tennis ball on the weekend.

Fanny Mairena
info@latinasenny.com
(917) 886-0074

Wendy Rodriguez

*"Love yourself, have dignity, know your worth
and don't settle."*

We are destined to win. We are born with a purpose.
I have three beautiful daughters who are my world, my right hand, my best friends and my biggest treasures. I am the CEO of Ultimate Sweat Zone Ladies and Kid's Fitness and the producer and host of Empowering Women TV and radio. But it's easier said than done.

It was 1998 and I was only 15 years old. I was pregnant with my first baby. In a blink of an eye, my whole world changed forever. Growing up in a macho, dominating society was challenging. Women really had no say in anything.

As a young girl, I saw my mother suffer in an abusive relationship, just like I heard my grandmother had. I was about 11 when she finally made the decision to leave my father. My mom had always being a devoted Christian and perfectionist, so in our house fornication and having kids before marriage was a sin. And there I was in an abusive relationship at 15, and pregnant. Everyone judged me and some spoke poorly about me, even family, church members and friends. My father, however, just completely disowned me. He didn't want to have anything to do with me or his grandchild.

Then, I found myself repeating the cycle. I turned 17 and got pregnant with my second daughter while on birth control! What a surprise for me, and one that God knows is my blessing from above. I suffered so much during that pregnancy. My baby's father was out cheating with different women while I was in the hospital giving birth. The phone rang. It was his mistress. So I was pushed to make the hardest decision of my life: to raise these two beautiful and healthy girls on my own and not repeat the cycle. I had to learn to love myself, to have dignity, to know my worth and not to settle.

As a teenager, I would never have imagined myself going to school, working full time and being a single mother of two. Because I let my emotions override my wisdom, I now had to face the consequences.

God has me covered no matter how hard the situation, no matter how overwhelming. I always feel protected by God and I believe he is going to make a way when there seems to be none. I always knew I couldn't give up. I was 18 and so blessed with his grace and favor. I was making over a thousand dollars a week, winning trips, electronics, and cruises while becoming the top sales person of the region and even the world. I did this many times, but the arguments and the threats from my daughters' father wouldn't let us live in peace. I was afraid for my life. I had to make another life changing decision; I transferred to Texas to work in the same field while I kept believing and dreaming.

WAKE UP CALL

One day, I was driving back from an amazing trip in Austin with a friend when a deer crossed the road in front of us. We swerved out of control and the car flipped many times. We hit a tree and landed in an eight-foot ditch. I was 19, bleeding, unable to breathe and in the back of the car not knowing how I got there. I couldn't tell where the tree ended and my seat began. The seatbelt was smashed between them. I was still conscious, not knowing how I got in the back seat of the car. I didn't know if we were going to make it out alive. My friend was badly injured but God gave her strength to crawl out of the ditch and ask for help. We were finally found! But we were too badly injured for them to help us at the local hospital and with no visibility, the helicopter was useless.

Our only choice was a hospital two hours away. The ambulance headed west. I couldn't see my friend. My lung collapsed, my shoulder was dislocated, my spleen was completely broken in half, and I had four broken ribs and internal bleeding. My rib punctured my lung. They inserted a tube to drain the blood. There was no anesthesia and they cut me open to save my life. When I woke up in intensive care, the only thing I can remember was telling my older brother, "Please take care of my girls!"

Two days went by and the pain became unbearable, worse than giving birth. I was ready to give up, when I received a phone call from a prophet. "I am going to heal you. I will raise you up. I am going to take you to the Nations and people will not understand how you got where I am going to place you," said Father God. Two hours later, I was out of intensive care. God healed me!

It was a miracle and I was thankful, but the whole process was overwhelming. Being a mom, a dad, a provider and a teen at the same time was a really hard task. I wanted to give up many times and go party, have fun and be like everyone else my age. But when I looked at my girls and knew that I was the only parent they could count on, I had to keep going. I knew that since God spoke to me, this tribulation would pass!

In 2001, I realized Texas was not for me and I moved back to Long Island. Two years later, I met the man I wanted to spend the rest of my life with. We wanted to do the right thing so we got married. He helped me raise my two girls and we were blessed with one other girl of our own. We could not have been happier. We were a very successful couple and at 22, we bought our first home and had two businesses. Financially, we were doing great. We were very involved in church, and a role model for couples. Our life was God, church and family.

THE HURRICANE

In 2006, after three happy years of marriage, a huge hurricane hit us. I started having a recurring dream. My husband would take us to the beach and all of a sudden, a huge hurricane would come. Even though our house was under water, no water would come into our home because we would drain it all out, so the water wouldn't harm us. It was so weird. I couldn't understand what it meant. One night, something else happened in the dream. I was standing right by my window and I said to myself, the hurricane is here.

The next morning, all hell broke loose. My husband asked me to move to Florida with him. He would move first, then the girls and I would follow after. I couldn't leave right away, because we had a business to tend to and I had to make sure I had staff to keep it running smoothly. I would travel to Florida once a month to be with him and sometimes I'd bring the girls. But something inside of me wouldn't allow me to move. People keep on telling me not to, that I would lose everything. So I keep on praying and asking God if it was his will to make it happen and if not, to please close every door. His word says ask and you shall receive, and I did!

I felt something different and I confronted my husband. "Are you seeing someone else?" I asked. (It's true what they say about women, we know when something is not right.) His reply was "yes". How can a man of God, who preaches about love and family, do this to us? I couldn't believe it. I was speechless. I was an emotional wreck. I didn't know what to do with my life. What would I tell my girls? How could I tell them? They were emotionally distraught and I couldn't do anything to take it away. And how can they not be, if the man they thought would be in their lives forever, a godly man, walked away with no explanation.

For two years, we didn't know where he was. We lost our

first home and we ended up living in a room in my mom's house. I remember sitting with my girls in that small room, and not knowing exactly what to tell them. Seeing the sadness in their eyes was heartbreaking.

WHAT COMES NEXT

I felt so uncertain about everything, and I had so many questions. The only thing I was sure about was that they needed me to stay strong. I had to find a solution, a solution that was going to determine our future for sure. I was 26 and left to raise three girls on my own. I was scared. I was a woman sitting in a room fighting for what she had left. I was a survivor.

Sometimes in our lives, hurricanes happen so we see the true colors in people. Yes, we feel hurt, disappointed or lied to. Yes, we lose hope and we lose faith. Yes, we feel there's no way out, no one to turn to, believe or to trust in. But never give up. With God, all things are possible!

When I look back at my life and remember how much we suffered, how much we struggled, the sleepless nights, the nights I cried myself to sleep, I think about how one wrong decision can affect the rest of one's life. I trusted that there was a reason. My divorce was the best thing that ever happened. It made me the woman I was supposed to be!

I am thankful for where God has taken me, grateful for my mom and the love and support of my sister and brothers. I am honored to be able to give back to my community and privileged to have the opportunity to empower and encourage women that are going through what I went through. We must never lose hope. There's always a light at the end of the tunnel. People can fail you but God never will. I am a witness to that! So don't give up on dreaming because if I had, I wouldn't be here telling you my story.

REFLECTION

1. Reflect on the hurricanes that have happened in your life. How did you get through them? Who was helping you?

2. Is God a part of your life? When has faith (in God or other forces) helped you through your struggles?

3. What are your blessings in life? Who/what are you willing to do anything for?

BIOGRAPHY

Wendy is a Guatemalan-American TV and radio host, producer, certified fitness trainer and instructor, entrepreneur, motivational speaker, and single mother of three beautiful girls.

Her TV Show, "Empowering Women TV", can be seen every Saturday via Alerta TV channel 463 Verizon Fios and every Tuesday on Radio Adonai 540 AM.

At age 26, Wendy established "USZ" Ultimate Sweat Zone and Kids Dance Studio", where she offers fitness and wellness for Women and kids. The studio was a top-ranked studio for three years before merging with Brentwood Community school and raising $6,000 for the school's graduates.

Wendy is a member of "SEPA Mujer, Hombres y Mujeres Cristianos de negocios", a community advocate for Long Island Headstart, a fitness and health instructor for Brentwood Community Schools, and a member of the Brentwood-Chamber of Commerce. She was nominated for Businesswoman of the Month from Mujer Actual magazine in 2011 and honored by legislators Monica Martinez and State Senator Phil Boyle for outstanding community work in 2014 & 2015. In 2015 she was recognized by Latina Exitosa, Latino Star, the Queens Courier/Star Network, and the NAACP as the Hispanic Heritage Month Honoree.

Wendy Rodriguez

(631) 398-1803

wendyrod1983@gmail.com

A LIFE OF WORTH AND GRATITUDE

Yai Vargas

*"When life hands you a difficult situation where you feel
undervalued and disrespected, be bold and brave enough
to know your worth."*

From the moment we are born, time passes quickly and we
move along with it. If we are lucky, we experience moments that
become a catalyst to map our journeys in life.

My moment was at the tender age of six at the New York
Auto Show. My dad would take my brother and I there religiously
every year. The more I went to the show, the more I became
enamored with the cars, and most memorably, with the Mercedes
Benz brand. I was so interested in the company, that when I was
to pick an internship at my university, I was determined to land a
position there.

The day that I applied, I was armed with three things: a
crisp resume, knowledge of every single Mercedes model and my
unwillingness to take no for an answer. I was a scared 20-year-
old girl with no experience, but I knew I wanted to be there. No,
I NEEDED to be there. Without an appointment, I requested
to meet an HR manager to introduce and sell myself to what I

hoped was an internship that I prayed existed. My plan worked.

I remember jumping out of bed for my first day on the job – I was an hour early. I made sure to give myself enough time to reach the office since it was a rainy morning. As I pulled into the parking lot, I could see the raindrops glistening on all the beautiful cars.

My experience included everything from drafting press releases on new models lines, to interviewing high-level executives on their recent promotions for the internal newsletter. I remember delivering Christmas toys to a local elementary school, bags and bags of donated toys that arrived with our surprise Santa in nothing less than the shiniest convertible. Yes, I said Santa and children's toys in a convertible in the middle of winter. I thought, could it get any better than this?!

It was three years into my position here when I started to incorporate my culture and language into the company. I was promoting diversity without really knowing it. I started asking why we weren't working with more Hispanic organizations, magazines or journalists and I even went as far as putting together my own marketing strategy for this market. Needless to say, the company wasn't ready for that step and this is when I realized I needed to pursue other opportunities where I could use my Spanish language – even if it meant leaving my dream job.

This internship was to change my life, not because of the actual job or task but because it opened my eyes to what was to become my biggest passion now: the Latino market.

USE WHAT YOU HAVE

When I was young and had already lived a few years in the U.S., I was so intrigued with mastering the English language and blending in that Spanish to me was an afterthought. However, my parents made it a point to always keep me fluent and never stopped practicing it at home. Knowing Spanish was the tool that I would use to set myself apart from my colleagues and classmates. I wanted to help companies and organizations learn to work with the Latino community. My responsibility was to share the Latino story.

I was not an expert on this subject by any means, so I dove into research about the different aspects, nuances, struggles and way of life of the Hispanic and the Latinos though books, articles and one-on-one conversations. This new world opened my eyes more and more each time that I spoke with Latino professionals and leaders in social gatherings at special events.

I truly enjoyed traveling and meeting people who were promoting capacity building, professional development, social change and political engagement – all for Latinos. All of these interactions slowly began to influence the work I was doing and would eventually begin to shape my networking career. By this point, I knew two things: I wanted to show companies how to work in the Latino space and I loved meeting Latinos who were doing significant work in that space.

During this time, I was lucky enough to be working on an account that would change my life. AIDS had never directly affected my life per se, but I specifically knew of one distant relative who was diagnosed years back. This organization was doing work that was directly impacting the Latino community. At first, I found myself drawn to the jarring statistics of our people and this global pandemic. Then I was moved by the raw stories of the people living with HIV/AIDS. It got real when my client lost his own battle with it. I began to reflect and realized I needed to share the great work this organization was doing by committing to fundraising via the connections I had made.

KNOWING WHEN TO WALK AWAY

There comes a moment in ones life when you learn to trust in your ability and get to know your worth. That moment for me came at a time I least expected it. My personal life couldn't have been better. I was in an amazing relationship, traveling the world and entertaining friends in a brand new luxury apartment I had just purchased overlooking the New York City skyline. I regularly attended some pretty extravagant galas with the likes of A-list celebrities and Fortune 100 CEOs. I was on cloud nine as they say.

All of the positive things happening in my world would soon be shadowed by an unfortunate sequence of events that occurred with a manager who would soon show me the ugly side of leadership – or the lack thereof.

I hated going to this job so much that I would drive past it everyday and wished that I would get into a car accident so that I would not have to go in. I was in a position where I didn't feel valued and knew I would never progress because of the way

I was being managed. If you are lucky, you will never encounter a bad boss, but if you do, one must take control and decide to move on. No one deserves to be undervalued. I decided to walk away from that by moving to a new industry and up to this day, it's the best thing that's happened to me professionally. From that experience, I knew what I wanted, needed and the type of environment I should be in. I had met so many people that loved what they did and loved where they worked. That inspired me to find it for myself. I wanted to feel like I did that first day I began at Mercedes Benz.

HUMBLED BY THE OTHER SIDE OF THE WORLD

A few years ago, I was blessed to have had the opportunity to travel to India for a friend's 4-day wedding. This elaborate union between two souls began with a short trip to a country that almost seemed like the complete opposite of what India felt like. Dubai is the epitome of opulence and luxury with the world's tallest skyscraper and gorgeous palm island; it feels as if you're in a dream of endless prosperity. Having seen the wealth that exists in Dubai, it's almost impossible to not be mesmerized by it.

Soon my short trip through Dubai came to an end and I was headed for the main event, India. Having been born in the Dominican Republic, I thought I knew what a third-world country was like and I thought I was prepared to experience it. As soon as I landed, India immediately made me think of New York City's Time Square except more crowded. It's almost impossible to imagine that, right? I don't get overwhelmed at much, having lived in such a crowded place for so long, but this was something I had never seen before. Add to that the fact that as my driver pulled out of the airport parking lot, we were sharing the road with elephants and cows! This was something else.

One of my favorite things in life is appreciating other cultures and languages across the world. I found myself internalizing the noise, smells, people, laughter, foods, and life around me. I also couldn't help but realize that I was thousands of miles away from home, near people who may never get to have the same feeling simply because they would never have the opportunity to leave their country.

India was the right combination of beautiful earth, struggle and vibrant culture. The country contains 1.2 billion people and the diversity among them is also clear to see. From the amazing wonders to the food and people to experience, this place taught me to appreciate others and the way they live. It makes anyone appreciate the smallest of luxuries that we take for granted, including running water, and the ability to have access to clean air and healthy food.

As I reflect on the experiences I have had, I think of how lucky I am to have seen so much in so little time. No matter how hard things have been in life, I stay humbled, motivated, and positive. I pride myself in having a positive attitude and always remember my travel through countries like India, where I experienced those who are less fortunate. I find myself reflecting on stories from those struggling with HIV/AIDS and think of how thankful I am to be in a position to help in some way. I am so grateful to simply be healthy. I learned that when life hands you a difficult situation where you feel undervalued and disrespected, be bold and brave enough to know your worth. One thing I know for sure is life happens and life goes on – the only thing we have is our health and our mutual respect. I hope to work with women who are both interested in professional development and who have the wish to help other women get ahead.

REFLECTION

1. Do you take the time to ask others how you can help them?

2. Do you know what your next step is in life or work?

3. Has your life ever been influenced by some place you have visited? How?

BIOGRAPHY

Yai Vargas is a Hispanic Marketing Executive who specializes in developing strategic marketing initiatives specifically focused on the Hispanic/Latino population and has experience in both corporate and agency. Her experience spans various industries including automotive, healthcare, sports, entertainment and currently financial services with New York Life. She studied Advertising and Marketing at the Fashion Institute of Technology and Integrated Marketing Communications at New York University.

As a self-proclaimed LinkedIn ninja and power networker, Yai founded Latinista, a Meetup group for Latina professional interested in professional and personal growth and holds monthly events with chapters in New York and Miami.

Yai is currently the National Latino Marketing Manager for New York Life Insurance where she is charged with implementing strategic marketing and recruiting initiatives across the US. She drives tactical programs promoting financial literacy and financial planning for the Latino community. She serves as a benefit committee member for The Latino Commission on

AIDS and is entering her eighth year in fundraising and social media for their annual fundraising gala, Cielo Latino.

Yai Vargas
yaindhy@gmail.com

Iris Soto

"Despite our challenges, we are always blessed."

Strength is the product of struggle. I was not aware of this at the age of 24 when my beautiful daughter Iraida was diagnosed with cerebral palsy when she was only eight months old. There is a quote that says, "Something as small as the flutter of a butterfly's wings can ultimately cause a typhoon halfway around the world". Nothing could have prepared me for the storm. Just like a typhoon, characterized by large masses of clouds, the direct force of this news slammed directly into me, causing extreme damage. The effects were devastating. Parts of me immediately fell apart. I succumbed to the false perception that my life no longer belonged to me.

A SPECIAL INSPIRATION

Raising a child with special needs has both its blessings and its challenges. The blessings come in forms of very small or very big and crucial victories--victories that we hoped would bring her one step closer, as much as possible, to being "normal".

The challenges evolved as she grew. I had to withdraw from my third year of college to care for her after countless surgeries and therapies. What I once considered my normal life was replaced by a more valuable commitment and dedication to the well-being of another human, my child.

Confrontation with depression, denial, fear, and the overwhelming daily needs of my child were the external realities of my life. The challenges that presented themselves daily left me feeling hopeless and isolated. And so in my mid-twenties, I had already completely loss myself. There was however, this child of mine. Every step, every achievement, every blessing and challenge became an amazing experience in our lives, even if most times I couldn't yet see through my pain. Our child demonstrated to us that everything is possible and so we dared to dream new dreams and push through the chaos. It wasn't that she was special, she made her parents special. She was exceptional! Then came our baby girl Blossom, who added joy to our lives. We became an exceptional family.

In 2003, my daughter who has special needs was in eighth grade. I was invited to her school one week before graduation where she was to receive four achievement awards. We were already so proud of her. Being a wheelchair user and having to overcome many obstacles did not keep her from persevering. The award event turned into something more than I could have ever imagined. Something that to this very day is still changing lives, including ours.

The Iraida Rosa Differently-Abled Scholarships were born the week of that awards ceremony. It initially derived from my pain as a mother. My special needs child was not acknowledged properly on the stage like all the other students. She was never called up and her awards had been placed on her lap instead. This discredited her efforts, in our eyes and hers, of all obstacles she had overcome in order to succeed, which is the premise of this now 13-year-old scholarship. We want to bring awareness that students with different abilities can rise to their highest potential, and their unique needs and learning styles should be valued and respected. It became my dream to someday bring this awareness to other schools.

I sat on that dream and others for many years throughout the pain and challenges. I pushed beyond my limits and pushed my family with me without direction, thinking, or shame. I kept pushing through chaos.

The combination of circumstances and bad choices took a toll on me for many years. I was never able to be vulnerable. I was led to believe that I didn't have a choice. I won't discount whether I knew or not that God had a plan for me. There was always hope and faith in my life and my dreams never left me. My dreams allowed me to smile. My tenacity was powerful. I lived with persistent determination and so our victories superseded our challenges. My daughter Iraida and I both obtained our college degrees.

WINNING FOR OTHERS

Flash forward to 2013 when I was invited to compete in the Bronx Puerto Rican Day Parade pageant. Again, I believed what others had told me — I was too old to compete. But my husband Rolando reminded me of the dream that I was sitting on--the one inspired by my daughter, the scholarship that would give recognition to the different abilities of students and send a message of inclusion and the importance of acceptance.

So I didn't hesitate to sign up for the pageant. I was proud of myself when I placed as first Adult Princess at the tender age of 48! I knew I had gained a platform! I will be heard! I will be seen! And I will be connected!

I knew I had work to do. I didn't have much confidence in myself but I had a whole lot of heart. This was a positive shift in my life. It motivated me. I started meeting the right people, going to the right places, and doing things that were more aligned to my dreams and passions. My outlook changed as well; my mantra was to no longer deny myself of any opportunities that came my way and to follow the direction of my dreams.

As I followed my journey, my passions and creativity started to emerge. I became an avid community activist. I always loved serving those in need and wanted others to do the same. My mom Carmen taught me that when you give, you always have. Despite our challenges, we are always blessed.

So I created the Friends of Iris Network so that others can serve their community and experience the amazing joy of giving and helping people in need. My 10 for 40 Rice Challenge, where my friends each donate 10 pounds of rice to feed 40 hungry men, women and children for Thanksgiving, have fed over 12,000 people in the last two years. I also set up drives, I walk for many worthy causes to bring awareness, and rally for rights and social justice. My greatest passion is advocating for children with special needs. My husband and I are polar bears who plunge into the icy waters of the Long Island Sound in an effort to raise funds to take special needs children to the Special Olympics. That warms our hearts. My family volunteers at the Ronald McDonald houses wherever we vacation and bring volunteers to connect with families of children being treated for illnesses. We are now the proud benefactors of two schools receiving the Iraida Rosa Differently-Abled Scholarships. We are looking forward to adding more schools in the future.

By honoring my mantra, my creativity started to blossom. There was a puppeteer, a singer, a lyricist, a painter, a writer, a speaker, and a film producer living inside of me as well. I say all this only to illustrate what was pent-up deep within me. I finally came to the realization that I had been living under the terms of others. As a family unit, we had conformed in a world not built for exceptional families. We had to learn to interact with a world that set us apart, marginalized us, and limited us due to ableism. We live in a world that assumes disability is always visible, and surrounds us with pervasive stigma. I won't deny there were also self-inflicted obstacles, as well as some caused by the actions of others with their own motives. Together, this combination sabotaged what would have otherwise been a more peaceful, happy and successful life's journey for me and my family.

I won't discount the blessing of having learned to overcome challenges. We learned that it's all about choices and that we have the power to create change. We learned how to draw out strength from our experiences and use it for personal growth and evolution. We built blueprints to assist us with new challenges as they arise. However, there was something missing in my life. As much as I engaged in activities that I loved, there was something screaming for my attention.

RISEN FROM THE ASHES

I had gone through life not knowing my full potential. So I decided to go on a journey of self-exploration. It was overdue. I wanted to discover who I truly was and how I could consciously make better choices and bigger changes. The more I explored, the more I discovered, and the more I discovered, the more I changed. The more I changed, the better choices I made, and the better choices I made, the more clarity I gained. I realized that there was unfinished business from my early life experiences..that I had been living in a prison made by myself. More importantly, it became clear to me that I had the power all along.

Then, as life has it, another major shift happened in our lives. It came in the form of a house fire on July 2, 2014, two days before our family vacation. After the fire and initial shock, I stood amidst what I perceived as chaos, again.

Surrounded by darkness, I looked around in disbelief at mom's charred room where the fire started. I was consumed by overwhelming sadness. I felt paralyzed as I looked around. For the first time, there were no thoughts on my mind. I just stood there and observed. There was a ray of light on the debris-filled floor that caught my eye and I followed it up. And there it was, sitting on the blackened window sill, a powerful and strange light that connected me to myself as soon as I laid eyes on it. I stood there in disbelief not knowing what I was confronting. I felt a sudden shift inside of me, as if something detached itself from me. I felt completely naked, unable to move. I wailed deeply, not understanding that I was having a spiritual experience. It was as if the universe opened up and somehow revealed my soul to me. There was an immense feeling of space and peace and courage within me, and at that moment, everything became possible. So I walked away and never looked back. I pushed the door open and stepped into my power. I knew in my heart that we would overcome this too.

We went back to basics. We had a long year of reflecting, accepting and embracing that without God, we are lost and without gratitude, there are no blessings. By turning inward, my family and I were able to overcome the aftermath of a home fire. During our challenge, we learned important individual lessons collectively. We value our lives and each other and embrace our vulnerabilities. We were able to express ourselves during our trying time more freely and honestly. We became closer and learned how to respect each other's views and accept that nobody has it all figured out. We do more of what we love. We focus on the greatness in each other and work on being more present. We accept that change is constant and look at our experiences with fondness. To quote Matt Smith, "We all change. When you think about it, we're all different people all through our lives, and that's okay, that's good, you've got to keep moving, so long as you remember all the people you used to be."

These fundamentals, along with my awakening experience, were the power that drove me into pursuing my life-long passion as a motivational speaker and facilitator. It became clear that motivating and inspiring others was the journey I wanted to take. Nothing else offers me such richness and joy than the passion to plant seeds of growth and awareness in those that are willing to receive it. Exploring self is a process that will unfold naturally at its own pace and set you free.

REFLECTION

1. What are some of the hardest challenges that you've faced in your life?

2. How did you react to the challenges you've faced in your life?

3. How did the challenges you've faced shape the person you are today?

BIOGRAPHY

Born in Puerto Rico, Iris is a proud Bronx, N.Y. resident where she obtained her B.S from Lehman College. She has been married for 31 years and is the proud mother of two adult daughters.

Iris is a motivational Speaker dedicated to the transformation of lives through her E.P.I.C (Exceptional Person In Charge) workshops of self-exploration and connection to what matters most. She's also the host of a monthly support group for parents with special needs children, where parents mastermind solutions, ideas, and reinforce self-confidence to become their child's best advocate.

She is the benefactor of The Iraida Rosa Differently-Abled Scholarships in two Bronx Schools. The scholarship recognizes the abilities of special needs students who have overcome obstacles in order to succeed.

Iris is an avid community advocate. She created the Friends of Iris Network where she conveys the power of giving to those who collaborate with her in an array of community-based events that bring support, supplies and empowerment to those in need.

Among several awards and distinctions, Iris is the honoree of a Humanitarian Award and serves on several organizations including Toastmasters International Public Speaking Club,

Brides Walk Planning Committee for Domestic Violence and Villa Maria Homeowners Association.

Iris Soto
irisjsoto@aol.com
(646) 805-8207

SELF CARE IS A FORM OF SELF-PRESERVATION

Kenia Nunez

"By teaching what I have learned through loss, I have empowered women to get strong physically, mentally and spiritually."

It was the evening of May 7, 2013 and I sat on my sofa, numb and waiting to speak to my three beautiful children, Marken, 13, Natalia, 9 and Ava, 5. One by one they sat down, and I could see in their faces that they knew what was going to come out of my mouth, but they waited for me to speak first. I took a deep breath, and prepared for the hardest thing I have ever had to do in my life. I looked my children in their eyes and just said it: "Your dad lives in heaven now."

Cancer came in with a vehement force. When I knew the battle would be lost, I prepared my children to the best of my ability, but nothing prepared me for those screams in the middle of the night from my five-year-old asking why God would take her daddy. I felt as if I were living in the twilight zone. I not only had to navigate through my grief, but also the challenging grief of my three fatherless children. I too, was fatherless. My mother immigrated to New York in 1970 and four years later, gave birth to me at the age of 17. My biological father had abandoned my mother when she was pregnant, but five years later, I would have a new daddy and a brand new baby sister.

MY INNER MONSTER

The word "daddy" never rolled off my tongue very easily. The harder I tried, the more difficult it was to say. If I didn't call my stepfather "daddy", then what would I call him? It was too late in the game to shift and call him by his first name, so I decided to call him nothing. He was not my father; I didn't have a father and was ashamed of the life we led behind closed doors. Every weekend was predictable at our house. First, he would play loud, depressing Spanish folk songs that pierced my ears like daggers. The drunker he became, the louder and more intense the music would grow. Loud music made me physically ill as a child. Not until much later would I discover how damaging it was to my spirit.

At just seven years old, I recall struggling with the thought that my stepfather was not a bad person, but a good person with a bad drinking problem. The abuse that I experienced was not physical, but emotional, and mental. It would transform me nevertheless. It was normal to have police cars outside of our home and police officers knocking down our door every weekend from the neighbors calling out of concern. It was normal for me to wet my bed at ten, and to plead the fifth when the "nosy" vecinos asked too many questions. The anxiety of seeing my mother's suffering, and the paranoia of not knowing what would happen when he had his next drink made me extremely vulnerable and scared. The fear also created my monster.

I was probably ten when my monster was born. I don't recall exactly when, but when she made her debut, I felt protected for the first time ever. She lived within, and came out when provoked, always enraged. She had no reasoning skills, she lacked compassion, and her only objective was to protect her master and destroy anything in sight with her venomous tongue. She wasn't violent, but if required, she prepared for any and all battles.

As the years passed, I became less afraid and more bothered by our living situation. I had been living on egg shells since I was 5. I was pretty fed up. I began retaliating by instigating fights with my stepfather that sometimes got physical. After an explosive encounter, I would top the evening off by calling the cops, having him arrested and then going out for a night of dancing. That was my secret life. To the rest of the world, I appeared like a polished, professional young lady; very few knew the other side of me.

When I was 17, I worked for worldwide, top-level companies. My thick skin helped me work under great pressure and since I had been raised in a battlefield, I was not really fazed by much. I also watched my mother work in a sweatshop and admired her greatly for her fortitude. My mom's dream for me was to become the first in our family to graduate college and work in an office, not a factory. Later on in my career, I chuckled, thinking that my mom's dream for me came true— I had indeed become the ultimate office worker.

FALLING IN LOVE

At 23 years old, I met Marlon. I had known him from the neighborhood, but now I saw him with new eyes. He was tall, handsome, with piercing green eyes, a contagious smile, and a jolly laugh. He was kind, compassionate, and had his own business at 23 years old. I knew he was the special man I wanted to spend the rest of my life with. Two months later, we moved in together. A year and a half later, I called him my husband.

I fell in love with Marlon's beautiful soul, impulsive spirit, and pure heart. However, all the things I completely adored in our early years were things I began to resent with each passing year. By 2008, we had three sweet children, a gorgeous house and he had three furniture businesses with an overhead of about $30,000 a month. Oh yes, then the stock market crashed...and so began the great decline.

By 2010, we were in a big financial hole and everything in our lives went from bad to worse. Marlon tried to keep his cool, even though we were behind on all of our personal and business bills. I wanted to take the burden from his shoulders, so I lied and told him my paycheck would cover the mortgage and more. Actually, I was borrowing money to pay our mortgage, and frantically charging my credit cards to cover the other household expenses.

As the year progressed, I noticed that he was now easily agitated, worried, and even on edge. He had three furniture businesses, employed many family members and friends, and felt he had a responsibility to keep the failing businesses open because so many people relied on him. I insisted he close all of the stores, fire everyone, and find himself a job, but he wanted to ride out the storm.

Due to his indecision, we grew quite distant. It was hard for us to communicate without arguing, especially about money. To avoid discussions with me, he would retreat to his "man-cave" where he would play obnoxiously loud music. Although he was not disturbing anyone else's peace, it brought me back to my childhood years where my stepfather's loud music was the haunting soundtrack of my life. Although Marlon and I had so many beautiful moments, this vicious cycle happened quite often; and when it did, my monster would emerge and attack without warning.

Eventually the monster turned against me. I had a mental breakdown, spewing poison so damaging that Marlon and I went months without talking. We did not talk of divorce, although sometimes I would make empty threats in an effort to get his attention. Soon those threats no longer worked, because he had shut me out of his life. I felt in my heart that divorce was inevitable, but he made it very clear that he would not leave his children. In fact, he became an even more incredible father as he realized the limitations of my mental state.

I turned to God on hands and knees. I wanted Him to fix things quickly, but I would soon learn he was grooming me to find inner peace in that very space of pain and anguish. I slowly began to realize that all the fear, anger, hurt, and rage from my childhood had been brought into my marriage from the moment

I said "I do". I realized that I loved that man more than anything and I had contributed immensely to the downfall of our marriage. I wanted him and my family back. I begged God for another chance at my marriage. I wanted to support, love, and lift him, not emasculate him as I had done for so many years.

God heard my prayers when our marriage entered a period of healing. I got a call from him. "Negrita," he said, calling me by his term of endearment, "you are one crazy woman but I love you and want to spend the rest of my life with you. We are going to make this work." Through my own tears and sniffles, I could also hear him crying. It took me eleven years of marriage to learn how to love unconditionally and live life in the present moment. I had my best friend back, just in time for our greatest test of all.

THE GREATEST TEST

Marlon was diagnosed with cancer in January 2012 and passed away in May of 2013. During that trying period, he became my greatest teacher as he secretly fought stage four cancer. He never felt sorry for himself, he no longer stressed about his business and he even decided to shut down two out of the three stores. He was carefree and happy despite his poor health. As he lost weight rapidly, many would question what was happening with him, and he would simply reply I have a "situation" with my blood, but he never mentioned his diagnosis. He treated cancer as if it were a common cold. When the doctors told him they no longer had treatment options for him, he walked away optimistically. This is when I realized the healing power of self-care.

Sometime in January 2013, the doctor shared that Marlon only had two weeks to live. I suggested that our family start practicing a holistic lifestyle by applying all the things that we learned from Marlon's chiropractor and the amazing holistic doctors we had met. We slept nine hours every night, juiced every day, took our vitamins, spent quality time together, created future goals, attended church, meditated, and practiced yoga. We were happy and at peace, despite Marlon's death sentence. Ultimately, he lived five months longer than the doctors anticipated.

After his death, I continued to practice the self-care we did together in his final months. I felt good and others around me noticed that I was quite strong and resilient given the situation. I had many people supporting me through my grieving period, but others asked me if I was "faking" my positivity, medicated, or just in denial over losing my husband. Instead of getting offended, I just accepted these comments as back-handed compliments. I quickly discovered that many women had a difficult time reclaiming their life after turmoil because they did not have the resources needed to do so. This need fueled my life purpose. The moment I realized how many women were overlooking their self-care was the moment I realized I wanted to spend the rest of my life teaching others what I had learned.

Practicing good self-care has helped me overcome depression, maintain a meaningful balance in life and help me heal from my past. By teaching what I have learned through loss, I have empowered women to get strong physically, mentally and spiritually, including my own mother who after 35 years of marriage, decided that she too was deserving of a better life.

The message is simple: self-care is a form of self preservation.

REFLECTION

1. Is there something that you need to surrender to God?

2. Are you allowing the "monsters" of your past to still haunt you today?

3. How can you practice self-care on a daily basis?

BIOGRAPHY

Kenia is a holistic health care coach that focuses on self-care from the inside out. After 20 years of working in corporate America, Kenia left what was comfortable to pursue her passion of helping other women find a meaningful balance in an ever-changing world. After her 37-year-old husband was diagnosed with cancer in 2012, Kenia became passionate about wellness. Just 18 months later, he lost his battle.

Kenia is the author of the life-transforming book, "Surrendering: When Pain is Transformed into Extraordinary Blessings", where she shares her thought-provoking story of being a young widow with three children. Her refreshing perspective on love, forgiveness, and surrendering is inspiring.

Kenia's mission is to spread awareness of the tremendous power of self-care, and the positive effects that it has on an entire family, community and the world. Through her self-care system SavvyMe, she passionately teaches the seven steps that helped her transform herself from powerless to empowered. Whether it's through virtual coaching, women's retreats, writing, speaking engagements or one-to-one encounters, Kenia's greatest passion is teaching women how

 to reclaim their life physically, mentally, emotionally and spiritually - one fabulous day at a time.

Kenia Nunez
coachkenia@gmail.com
(917) 361-1324

Yaneli Sosa

"Believing in yourself and fighting for your dreams is what enables you to live each day and face every obstacle."

I left the tabonuco, the drum, the gallons of water, the stained bananas, the stench of burning, the fire, and the misery of those who did not dream, in order to follow my dreams.

I was encouraged by my grandmother, who always told me, "Nele, you have to grow and get out of here and help your mom get ahead so your dad does not hit her so much, otherwise one day he will kill her." And so with those words echoing in my head, I grew desperate to have my own voice to confront my father and demand that he not hit her anymore. I no longer wanted to live that horror movie. I grew up and faced him, and today there are no more blows for my mother.

The poor woman has healed from the verbal abuse; now she does not pay attention to what my father tells her. Believing in yourself and fighting for your dreams enables you to live each day and face every obstacle. Allow yourself to dream, whether you are twelve, thirty, forty, fifty or eighty- it is just a number. Your willpower is within you and believe me, I am the fruit of that labor.

THE FIRST HURDLE: FAMILY

A friend of the family managed to get me a scholarship with DJ Gordy, who is a very famous radio personality in the Dominican Republic, to study speech. When he heard me speak, he told me that he was going to help me. He said he loved my voice and believed I had a great future in locution.

Now you can imagine the emotion I felt, until I found out that my aunt, who lived next to him, had told him, "Why are you going to give her a scholarship when she is just a little farm girl? She will not appreciate it." As if to say I was an idiot with no future. But thank God he did not listen to her and said to me, "In this career, you will find many obstacles. The first will be your family, and you have to work hard to show your talent." Finding out what my aunt had said to him hurt so much because I thought, "What harm am I doing to her by trying to better myself?" As fate would have it, a few years later, I had to receive her at my house where I lived very comfortably thanks to my work, which she had almost stolen out of my little hands. I love my aunt, but this experience serves as an example of how family can hold us back. Sometimes our families do not want to hurt us; they just want to protect us from struggle or failure.

I waited anxiously for my school classes to finish so I could go to Santiago for the weekend to take my speech classes. My mom spent the entire week reminding my dad that he had to give me money for the fare, otherwise I would have to stay at my beautiful Aunt Milagro's house. I loved it there because my cousins lent me their clothes, did my makeup for me, and took me on strolls around town where I simply looked, listened, and learned.

I knew there was something more than the countryside and the city of Santiago, which is how I came to the capital Santo Domingo and saw all those big buildings and lights. I thought I was daydreaming, because in the countryside where I was born, there were no lights, and we had electricity maybe three times a week.

Every day in the capital was like a dream come true. One of those dreams was when I met Don Corporán de Los Santos, a legend of Dominican television. I was nervous and frightened because I admired him so much, ever since I was little. I wanted him to give me the opportunity to work with him, and that is what happened. Every program at his side proved that dreams can come true, because I used to watch him as a child on the television, and now I was working with him.

Those achievements made me forget the bad times I went through, like when I had to walk kilometers on foot to reach my old job where I was a paralegal because I needed the money to support myself, or when my aunt told me I had to move out of her house.

That day, I felt that the sky fell on me because I did not know the names of the streets well, and was guided only by the signs. It was like "moving the cushion out from underneath me", as I like to say. Now I see that she did me a favor, but it took me a while to recognize it and stop being angry about it. Soon afterwards, I became totally independent and paid my rent in

Mrs. Carmen's pension, next to the school. There I met girls like me, hungry for improvement. I remember living in a room that was so small, I had to bend down to enter it. You could not get two people in the room because they did not fit unless they were sitting together on that little bed of wood, which I thought of as my presidential bed. I could not see otherwise because I had so much hope and security in all my goals and projects that I knew it was something temporary. I wove my dreams like a cobweb-slowly, but firmly. It does not matter what the path is like if you have a clear purpose. Enjoy the little things in life so that you may savor and appreciate the big things.

In my country, I was the image of big-name advertising campaigns and appeared on major television programs and the internet. This was incredibly satisfying, and thousands of people saw me and followed my work. However, they saw something in me that I did not. They all considered me very pretty, while I did not, although it seemed otherwise. I was not the kind of girl who would have plastic surgery on her breasts and waist, unlike most of my colleagues. It was all part of my personal growth to realize that I'm beautiful and perfect in the eyes of God. If at any moment I decide to get some cosmetic surgery that is fine, but that is because I decide to and not because society demands it.

HELLO NEW YORK

Then my little dream bug told me there's another place for me where I could get my loved ones ahead more quickly. I came to New York with my dreams, goals and the strength and support of my family (my mom Nero, my dad Fermin, my brothers Gustavo, Evelina, and my nephews Chaveli Tirson, Winton, Eliut, Cherlin, Arolfi, Alinson and Alexander). They believe in me more than I do myself; they are my inspiration and my engine, along with television, which is how I inform and inspire so many people.

New York not only welcomed me despite the language barrier, but also helped me adapt to being away from my family, friends and a personal lifestyle of comfort. Now I was living a completely different way of life. I was sleeping on furniture, which I knew I would have to leave eventually because as friendly as people are, they do not let you stay more than six months at their house. After a couple of weeks, you have to start paying the bills. I went from driving my car to taking the train, and from national television to local television. For me, these were drastic changes.

However, this same local television experience that helped me get to know my Latino people, and how important and influential we are in this country. It also motivated me to continue bettering myself. I began to study English and then transferred my credits to a university here. I currently appear on a stable television program where I am interviewing personalities from the artistic and political world in the Big Apple.

Step by step, I am forging my future without giving up my present-- a present that at one point was carried away by my lack of self-esteem and loneliness disguised as love. There I was, come undone, my sad little heart broken, but I went back and got up because I could not forget what I had come here for. That is what keeps me standing today.

In the city that never sleeps, it is very easy to become a bit apathetic and cold, especially if you do not work on your spiritual side. I've always been connected with something very special that is in the hereafter. I call it God, but others may call it Allah or Buddha. The important thing is to believe in something that gives you peace and quiet. In my personal search for this, I began going to spiritual retreats. I am not referring specifically to religious retreats. I mean a place where one goes to meditate and reflect on daily life, personal identity, and answers to questions about life consequences and choices. When we are silent within ourselves, we discover the answers to these questions and that is why I recommend retreats, at least once a year. Meditation, bikram yoga, and eating healthier are also important in this new lifestyle. When you are in search of your personal welfare without harming anyone, everything changes for you. You no longer get angry so often. When someone speaks out, for example, you realize that person is just looking for a way to get your attention or to have his needs be heard.

YOUR PLACE IN THE UNIVERSE

Fight! Never get tired. My life is like yours, with ups and downs, but you just have to stay focused and love yourself. Give all that love to others because that will keep you happy. As they say, we give, we receive, and if we love, that's what we'll receive. And when you feel sad, cry. But then say to yourself, "that's enough" because we must continue with our heads held high.

Remember that God made a universe for you and it conspires 100 percent in your favor. Be careful what you think because you will attract it to your life. Think positive things, those things that make you happy. I think, for example, of the sincere and sweet smile of my nephew Eliut. I get happy and laugh like a child, I read self-improvement books, especially the Chilean author Jules Bevione, and I read biographies of people I admire. I invite you to practice some of these techniques and learn well as they did. See that you can do things too, that nothing is impossible. On the contrary, everything is possible. If you're alive, then you're winning.

Let's go! Think no more. What you want is within walking distance of you: Goal + Focus + Action = Results. Happy and fulfilled. Do it and remember this formula always. It works!

REFLECTION

1. What positive things can you think of in your life that make you happy?

2. What techniques for self-improvement do you practice? How can you learn to love yourself?

3. How can you become a leader of the pack? What leadership skills do you possess?

BIOGRAPHY

Yaneli Sosa (Neli) is a famous television personality from the Dominican Republic. Born in Moca, Yaneli always had the gift of gab and an outgoing personality. After graduating college, she began her career in media through modeling, and placed third in the 2006 "Miss Dominican Republic Earth" pageant. She went on to become the face of major campaigns such as Santo Domingo coffee and Ars Health. Yaneli then represented her country in the "2008 Space" in Mexico, where she learned from radio and television experts. She returned to her homeland and became a TV reporter for "Controversial Leila" and the Presidency of the Dominican Republic before beginning an acting career.

In 2011, Yaneli hosted the hit TV show "Sabado De Corporan", co-starring Don Corporán De Los Santos. In 2012, Yaneli moved to New York City and established herself in American television, appearing on "El Cafecito" and "La Hora", broadcast on World Fox.

In 2014, Yaneli became co-host of the New York-based "AquiTV", broadcast through "Super Canal Caribe" and she was presenter of the year for "La Prensa NY" in 2015. She is currently the face of Josephine Completo Spa NYC, and models for celebrity make-up artist, Paolo DiValdi.

Yaneli Sosa

yanelisosa20@gmail.com

(646) 496-2194

Nenci Rodriguez

"Strive to be a person of value, and success will undeniably follow."

Being in sales and the media communications world has made me overcome negative beliefs that were formed at an early age. It has been the voice inside me- the voice of perseverance, determination, and faith-- that has pushed me to overcome the obstacles I've experienced. As I look back, the difficult times in my life have become my biggest lessons. And interestingly enough, the values and principles I was taught have become the foundation of my life and career.

I was born in a small town in Mexico, into a family of ten siblings, where I enjoyed my childhood and played freely with other kids from the same town. I was careful to get good grades; it wasn't hard for me because I loved school. I used to enjoy when the teacher would ask my best friend and I to help other students who needed assistance with assignments or homework. I still get a sense of satisfaction when I can help someone. However, my life changed when my parents decided to migrate to the United States.

SCHOOL STRUGGLES

We came to a small town in Texas where I was placed in the fourth grade. As I stared at the huge school compared to the little one I knew in Mexico, I panicked, my stomach ached, and I couldn't keep tears from rolling down my cheeks. I was terrified. I didn't know the language and at that time, there weren't that many Spanish-speaking students in school. How I remember their irritated faces when they were asked to translate for me. Affected by the change of culture and language, my mind would wonder off, longing to be in my old, familiar, small classroom back in my country. It would bring tears to my eyes, making me miss class and almost having to repeat the grade.

"Why are the kids staring at me?" I thought, not realizing I had been wearing the same clothes for multiple days. Not only did the students notice, but my teachers did too. One morning, I walked into the classroom and bags of clothing, that the teachers had asked the students to donate, were lined up for me. Embarrassed, but simultaneously happy, I accepted the bags. I was thrilled to receive my very first used gym shoes given to me by my classmate Brittany. They were semi-new and were a tad big on me but to me they were new. I wanted to express my gratitude but couldn't in English. All I did was look at her and smiled, hoping she would understand.

Even after that nice gesture, I was determined to convince my mom that I wanted to go back to my old school and friends. Sitting in the school office, I would see her frustration when she would have to pick me up from school because of my distress. It was a victory for me since she'd have to take me to her adult English classes that I so enjoyed. The ladies were fun and entertaining; I would sit and listen. I learned so much from listening! I enjoyed being around mom's friends and neighbors and I felt safe around them. As I grew older, I realized they had so much experience and wisdom. I now know how many "life coaches" I've had throughout my life that I didn't even recognize as "coaches".

Math and Art were the only classes where English was not needed. I was determined to learn English quickly so I could answer on my own and be able to defend myself. So that's what I did. It was fun learning to speak a second language and I'm fortunate to have had the opportunity to learn and live a different culture without forgetting about my own.

My father, although a nice man, was strict and an alcoholic, which at times made the environment at home very tense. The first time I saw the school band play, I knew I wanted to be part of it. The soft, relaxing sound of the saxophone would transport me to places where the brightness of the sun could bathe me incessantly. But all I received was a bold "no" from my dad when I pleaded with him for permission to join the band. Not giving up, I asked to be on the volleyball team. I grew up playing volleyball and loved it, but because I would have to stay after school, he again said no. I now wonder if volleyball would have been a free ride to college for me. I will never know. As you can imagine, I grew up with almost no friends due to my father's strict rules.

Sophomore year in high school I started working part time

at a Mexican restaurant. Seeing all my classmates eat and drive off while I was waiting tables made me feel encapsulated. Having no transportation that summer, I asked my father to teach me how to drive, and he responded by saying "Pa que quieres saber?" (Why do you want to learn?).

My plan after graduation was to move to Chicago and attend college. At that moment, I made the decision to combine my junior and senior year of high school to finish early. My brother laughed at my decision but I proved him wrong and fulfilled one of my first, fearless goals.

The same day I graduated from high school, my younger sisters graduated from eighth grade. My father was working and didn't plan to attend, and my mother couldn't drive so she couldn't go either. Without telling my mother, I took a deep breath, grabbed the keys and drove to their graduation. That same evening was my high school graduation ceremony. Heartbroken, I heard my mother talk my unwilling dad into finally going to the ceremony. I was done with high school!

THE JOURNEY CONTINUES

I came to Chicago ready to fulfill my hopes and dreams. At first, I was intimidated by the big city but with my newborn freedom, I was ready to explore.

The first thing I did was try to register for college. However, I was unfamiliar with the application process and became frustrated and discouraged. The university kept requesting more paperwork and I was getting desperate to make some money and pay tuition.

My mother and my younger siblings also moved to Chicago with me and having seven people squashed into a three-bedroom apartment was challenging. We had too many expenses and not enough income. My dream of college had to wait.

With some guidance, I would have probably received financial aid and attended college, but instead, I decided to look for a job. However, I always promised myself that I would go back to school as soon as I got settled. I took the first job I was offered, but knew I could do better so I kept searching. I was 17 when a bank called just a month after I applied. I started working full time.

I also had training in media communications, specifically radio, and I loved it but couldn't survive financially on a beginner's salary. I decided I would do radio as a hobby.

Then I was introduced to the mortgage banking industry. I liked the impact that the mortgage company made in people's lives when they helped them buy their home. I was offered a job as an opener. My manager, Marisol, was a single mom, very successful woman and my very first mentor. I will forever be grateful to her. She taught me much of what I know today, believed in me when I doubted myself, and saw in me what I couldn't see. Working under Marisol gave me the opportunity to educate myself and she was committed to teaching me the art of sales and mortgage banking. I saw it as a challenge and an opportunity to help people and educate clients on one of the biggest financial decisions they would ever make.

After working for a year as an opener, I received the worse call one can receive. My father had died suddenly of a stroke. That morning, my heart stopped. I was distraught. It had been four years since I had seen my father, who I loved and missed. I remember thinking "this is so unfair". I never took the chance to tell him how much I loved him. For many years, this feeling of incompleteness haunted me. Interestingly enough, when I returned from burying him in Texas, I brought renewed courage and determination. To me, it was a gift he left to me. I wanted to honor his memory. I was no longer hesitant in my decisions; I went into Marisol's office and told her I wanted to become a mortgage banker, even though I would lose my salary and have to work on 100 percent commission. His death made me realize how fragile life is and how important it is to be bold and live life. I know he watches over me.

One of my fearless goals was to buy a house for my mother. She had never owned her own home and I was determined to make that wish a reality. However, I also felt I had failed myself for not finishing college and I was still only 22 years old. It was bothering me so much that I asked a colleague of mine what he thought. He responded, "We make more than people with master's degrees. I don't think it's necessary." His answer gave me peace of mind but did not quite silence my desire to return to school.

Eventually, I returned to school for a year but had to stop once again after I bought the house, which was another fearless goal accomplished. I told myself I would finish school regardless of how old I was. I would not leave it halfway completed.

GRATITUDE IN CHALLENGING TIMES

In 2007 and 2008, the recession hit. The country's housing market crashed. The "economic bubble" burst, and immediately housing prices declined to new lows. Foreclosure rates skyrocketed and led to a crisis in mortgage and credit markets, affecting my business tremendously. It was difficult to provide mortgage loans or refinances. However, my spirit of gratitude and faith kept me afloat. I made it a point to count my blessings in spite of my situation. Instead of giving up, I decided it was the perfect time to continue my education. I enrolled in school again and was committed to finishing my degree. I spent some summers studying inside and giving up time with friends to prepare homework assignments. After sacrificing my social life, working and going to school full time, I finally graduated, making me the first in my family with a college degree. I sometimes ask myself "was the sacrifice worth it?" I honestly can say it was.

In the past 14 years, I've helped many families and young adults move into their own homes. It's been important to me to become a person of value rather than a person of success. I build strong business and personal relationships based on four pillars: respect, trust, service, and commitment. These principles, I believe, have made me a successful and trusted professional, along with the guidance I received from great mentors in my life. Furthermore, I am a co-host on a Spanish radio program because to this day, media communications is still one of my greatest passions.

I am very grateful for all the opportunities and challenges I've had. These experiences have stretched my comfort zone. It is in the moments of despair that we find the courage and strength to achieve our fearless goals. They allow us to continue our journey in life and create our own road map for success.

REFLECTION

1. Can you identify people you admire and see as role models that could become your mentors?

2. What is your greatest fear and how can you overcome it?

3. What are you grateful for that you take for granted?

BIOGRAPHY

Nenci was born in Mexico and came to the U.S. at the age of eight. She lived in Texas before settling in Chicago. Nenci has 14 years of experience in sales and in the mortgage industry as a Sr. Mortgage Banker, which has helped her create lifelong business relationships. She has also had the opportunity to be part of assisting thousands of individuals and families in buying their homes.

Nenci has an educational background in business administration and marketing, as well as certification in radio. She is currently a co-presenter for an online radio program which provides positive news and information on such topics as women, culture, art, community services, business, and education. Nenci is passionate about women's empowerment and is a fire-walker graduate. She holds certifications in NLP (Neurolinguistic Programming), Emotional Intelligence, and Pastoral Leadership (Liderazgo Pastoral), which has enabled her to teach third grade religious education.

Nenci Rodriguez
Nenci@sbcglobal.net
(773) 330-3824

Mayra Betances

"Those who truly care for you will linger, accept and understand you."

"Perhaps a deep coma will work to make the pain go away. Look. That corner after the light is a good one. You won't crash into any other cars and you will be injured enough to sleep through it all…"

These were my thoughts as I drove to work on the morning of Aug. 20, 2014. These are thoughts I never would have expected to have.

I had a relatively good life with three children, a husband, a job, and a business in the making. I was also continuing my college education, active in social issues and very involved in community events. I had good health and a supportive family. Perhaps I had too much too soon.

I'm one of seven children and the first in my family with a college degree. I emigrated from the Dominican Republic at the age of 12. I come from a very strong and close family. My biggest motivation is my mom, Felicia Betances, who taught me resilience and generosity through her story. My biggest pride is my dad,

191

Ydebrando Betances, who taught me integrity and accountability through his character. I got married at 17, becoming a wife and a stepmom.

I had my first child at 19 and I continued my education while building my business and returning to work full time. Our family grew when I had my two younger children six years later.

THE DARK DAYS

The business took a toll on me and was overwhelming, mainly because I wanted to do it all, all of the time. Meanwhile, the children were in constant need of attention and my husband worked all the time, leaving no time for our relationship.

By this time, I was in my early 30's and life was chaotic. I was continually disappointed by what I saw as my husband's lack of ambition; nevertheless, I've never met a more noble man. We mutually agreed to separate before things got too unpleasant for our family.

So here I was, a single mom with a good job, taking the last few credits needed for my degree in communications. The kids were healthy and all had good grades, so I decided to focus my business on the area that I loved the most, which is paper crafting. This left room for relaxation and quality time with the children.

In 2013, my children's father decided to move out of state against my wishes, but he argued he could provide better for the kids if he moved and so he did. Now this left me completely in charge of absolutely everything. This was the hardest and most challenging time in my life.

On the morning of Aug. 20, I kept telling myself in an inner voice to go and crash my car onto the side of the road. As I approached my exit, I became anxious that I was running out of enough speed to crash, and how dare I fail at this too. This was my last thought when I realized I was at the parking lot of my job. I got out of my car and started my daily walk through the plant where everyone religiously gave greetings every morning. By this time, I was conscious enough to notice they all had a strange face as I passed by and it wasn't until I got to my cubicle when I noticed my shirt stuck to my chest like glue. I looked down and saw it was wet…as if I had been bathing in it. It was my tears. Tears that were still running down my face and I was not feeling them.

I grabbed my phone and texted my friend and told her I had some thoughts and I needed to talk. She called me and told me to talk to someone at my job that could help or to go to the hospital but not to be alone. I wanted to harm myself enough to put life in idle, because that was what I thought would calm all my hurting, loneliness, and financial troubles.

IN IDLE MODE

My eldest son Luigi was nearing the end of his middle school years and was now struggling with his grades. The school and I worked to get him a mentor for daily meetings throughout his last two years in middle school. He almost didn't move on to high school with his class. This was a frustrating and stressful time for me, as I wanted my son to be responsible, and set an example for his younger brother and sister.

Meanwhile, my younger ones, Deogo and Ella, always did their homework and got A's and B's. My middle child Deogo has ADHD and we had to give him his medicine every morning before school. I remember we didn't want to, but the child was getting D grades across the board. We were also receiving numerous complaints at parent meetings with the district counselor and principal because of his constant class disruptions and need for attention. We gave in and decided to try it. It turned out to be the best thing we ever did for him. He immediately focused and everything fell into place for him. He made the honor roll two years in a row and was able to play soccer in a traveling team to everyone's delight, including his own.

Ella, my daughter, has always been my trooper. She knew where everything was in the house, helped with the boys as if she was the oldest, and kept her grades up. She was in dance school and always crafted with me. She is an inventor at heart, and even developed a tendency to write poems and verses, which she continues to do today.

I, on the other hand, was trying to juggle it all on my own, because as women, we are natural caregivers and I always thought I was "Wonder Woman" and could do it all. I was working 8:30-5, five days a week, in a demanding position at an engineering company that needed my full and undivided attention. I received endless calls from school and I had to literally walk out of my job to attend to whatever the situation was with the kids. I was also trying to finally finish college, taking classes online while also building my business.

Money was tight and even though I was receiving the agreed upon alimony, I was falling short. I had all the kids in sports and extracurricular activities. Food and bills were outrageously high and I was not on any government assistance. On a personal and spiritual level, I was experiencing situations that affected me deeply, which only added stress to my already shaky situation.

I was battling with emotional issues, an ugly and frivolous breakup, a lawsuit with my preceding landlord, and a financial situation that got worse by the hour. I was alone, personally hurting, financially shaken, away from my children and frankly, torn to pieces. My life, dreams, ambitions, and joy had been practically shattered in a matter of one year.

INTO HIGH GEAR

So here I was…admitting to myself that I was deeply depressed and needed medical treatment. I was diagnosed with severe depression and anxiety. The treatment included prescription pills for anxiety and depression and weekly emotional and psychiatric therapy. I began right away and my family was there every day, making sure I was well and ready to take on my life again. When my children were on vacation with their father, my sister came and stayed with me so I would not be alone.

I went back to work after a two-week break and tried my very best to move forward and put all positive vibes out to the universe for my prompt recuperation. During this healing time,

I continued prayer sessions with a dear friend who I appreciate immensely. My children came back and it was like the sun came out. Yes, I still had to go to court and yes, I still ended up paying some fees and enduring more emotional distress and disappointment at every turn, but I was now in control. I had the support of my family and my dear friends who I consider to be my shield from my own self-destruction during turbulent times. My children rejoiced in bringing home good grades and handmade art which they knew I would love. My husband and I grew closer, and I had a few angels in my life who came to me at a time of need with no interest other than to see me well and back on my go-getter track. They believed in me because they could see what I could become while I was blinded by the fog of my own personal war.

I decided to go back to what I was about, to being myself, attending networking events and learning about women in business. At one event, I learned about a woman who was a writer for a magazine. I always loved to write poems, stories, passages and of course, I'm a blogger of art and lifestyle at my core. I was not able to meet the woman then, but I was able to stalk her on social media and reach out through blogging about a product she had just released…a planner! She immediately saw my ability and thanked me for the write-up.

We connected and she became my business mentor. Her group, ETTWomen, provided me with a platform for my business life and introduced me to rare opportunities. I joined the group and my business and personal life soared! Why? Because

I connected and mingled with likeminded women that were passionate about entrepreneurship. These women supported my business as friends couldn't, because they simply could not relate to my business journey. I moved away from negativity, paid no attention to drama, and distanced myself from people who dragged me down.

I'm back to who I've always been: active, innovative and very much socially involved. I completed my credits and got my college degree, thanks immensely to my parents. My business is a profitable and successful one. I was awarded the ETTWomen in Business Start-Up of the Year in 2015. My company has created invitations for well-known corporations and famous New York magazines, like BELLA NY. In 2015, my work was recognized by the one and only Lisa Vanderpump. I was presented with the offer to lead a chapter of my women's group. I'm now launching a third chapter in Columbus, Ohio. I also founded a non-profit organization, whose mission is to create happy childhood memories for unprivileged children in the Dominican Republic through a cultural exchange. I now live in Ohio with my husband and children, and I'm medication free and thriving personally and professionally.

The lesson that I've learned from this journey is that there truly are negative people who will harm you as you search for happiness and prosperity. In the end, they are just fighting their own war and one should feel only great sorrow for these lives, for they do not know life without misery. I learned that depression hurts and that the more I ran away from confronting a situation, the more damaged I became, but perhaps the remedy was time and distance. I also learned to detect dishonesty by its character. There is no closure…there are just multiple ways to process a story in your life to shift into high gear. Those who truly care for you will linger, accept, and understand you.

Finally, if you are a dreamer, check yourself for grit and charisma to give you fearlessness, and passion to lift you out of despair into a positive state of believing!

REFLECTION

1. Are you in idle or high gear? How can you get to high gear?

2. What do you have to truly lose to be yourself?

3. Who in your life can raise you from despair?

BIOGRAPHY

Mayra Betances is the CEO and founder of the award winner company D&E Papel, a Stationery and paper product brand. Betances is also an arts and lifestyle blogger which she publishes on dandepapel.com Betances migrated to the New Jersey, U.S. in 1992 from the Dominican Republic and now resides in Columbus Ohio along with her family of 3 children and her husband; Betances desire for growth and determination to make a stand as an example for herself, children and Latinas, helped her get a College degree in Communications. Poised on giving back, in 2009, Betances started a community project collecting used Halloween costumes; aimed for the underprivileged children in the Dominican Republic to celebrate their heritage through this cultural exchange, Betances founded this project as a not for profit organization in 2015 and named it Create Happy Moments, becoming it's CEO and Director of the Board. Betances is the Columbus Chapter Leader of ETTWomen, a community of likeminded women and entrepreneurs dedicated to supporting and educating each other while growing their businesses. A member and Content Curator

of Latinas in New York; an online powerhouse group with over 4 thousand members.

Mayra Betances
mayra@dnepapel.com
(201) 888-0576

Maria Teresa Ramos & Sandra Ramos-Magnani

"Positive things can come from painful experiences."

Most people know us as sisters. What few people know is that we did not grow up that way. Maria Teresa is actually Sandra's aunt, but she is only two years older than Sandra. Her brother, Jose De La Luz, is Sandra's father. It was America that made us sisters.

One of our dearest memories was when we were only three and five years old, both living in Mexico. We played with dolls and water at the family home in the picturesque, mountain village of Las Iglesias, Tepehuanes in the Sierra of Durango. Another great memory was Sandra's First Communion celebration. Sandra was eight years old and had come from America to see us. That was the last time we were together in Mexico, but we never dreamed we would one day be together in America.

GOODBYE MEXICO

It all started on one-life-changing night when Maria Teresa was only 11. Her happy life as the youngest of eight children was shattered when she was awakened in the middle of the night by a family friend. Her mother had been sick with complications from diabetes. Maria Teresa knew something serious had happened, but she dared not ask what it was. The family friend hurried her and her older sisters into the car and they set off for the neighboring town. It was an ominous, four-hour drive through the dark mountains. Maria Teresa remembers the quiet and the dark of the night closing in, accompanying her feeling of dread that the worst had actually happened. She dared not ask where they were going or why. Instead, she looked up into the beautiful, star-studded sky. The stars seemed extra bright tonight, almost alive. She began to wonder…is my mother already up there, watching over me?

The blanket of night had broken into the reddish blush of dawn when the car finally reached its destination. Maria Teresa noticed several people dressed in black wandering in town. "If my mom is here, could she be dressed like this?" Maria Teresa thought. The car pulled up to a home that was once owned by her mother's sister, but was vacant now that she was living in the U.S. She walked to the door and when she opened it, Maria Teresa saw her mother in a coffin and her grief-stricken father standing nearby. In shock and sorrow, she ran to his arms, nestled her head against his chest and listened to his heart and his emotions as they embraced. "We are now alone," she said to him, and for the first time in her life, Maria Teresa saw her father cry.

Sandra was not at the funeral, but her father was. He was Maria Teresa's brother, Jose, who was 22 years older than Maria Teresa, who had come from the U.S. to pay his respects. Maria

Teresa also remembers seeing another tall, young man walk up to the casket and gaze lovingly at her mother for a long time. "He must really have loved her," Maria Teresa thought. Then she realized it was actually her brother Jesus, who she had not seen for some time. He had made the trip from Las Vegas to be with the family.

Maria Teresa always had an optimistic side that looked for the silver lining in any situation. She always said that even in her most painful moments, God has always been at work creating a greater plan. She believes God works in mysterious ways through others around you. Here, in the midst of her grief, there was a ray of light. Jose was there with his wife, Catalina (or Cata, for short), who has been a loving angel in Maria Teresa's life and a great influence on her. Jose turned to Maria Teresa and asked if she would like to come with him and Cata to live in the United States. Little did Jose know that at one point in her life, Maria Teresa had dreamed about being in the U.S., sharing moments with his family! Deep down, Maria Teresa had always yearned to live there, but thought it was not to be. Now, instantly, with a firm resolve that seemed to come from up above, Maria Teresa answered yes. Her father easily consented to the plan, feeling that America was a better place for her to be. Within a week, Sandra and Maria Teresa were together in America, living as sisters in one family.

TEACHERS AND FRIENDS

Sandra was a child who believed everything was possible,

and you couldn't convince her otherwise. She always had a good reason, solution or excuse for everything and Cata used to say she'd make a great attorney someday. When Cata would ask her to help around the house, Sandra would eventually give in, but not before she let her know the well thought-out reasons for her reluctance. Cata told Sandra nobody would want to marry her if she didn't learn how to cook or clean, but Sandra had a different plan. She wanted to go to college to get a degree and then a job that paid so well she could afford to eat out and hire someone to clean her house!

Life was good, but Sandra had her doubts and insecurities. She lived with the constant struggles and fears of being in a family of undocumented immigrants. Sandra remembers playing outside with friends and running to hide behind the bushes when the UPS truck came by. What if it was immigration? What if she was caught and sent back to Mexico? Sandra had heard stories of life in Mexico from her relatives. Living there would have ruined her plans for the future.

Of everyone in the house, Sandra spoke the best English, so she was the voice for the family. She dealt with the banks, schools, utility companies, salespeople, doctors, creditors, bosses, etc. on the family's behalf. When more relatives emigrated from Mexico and lived in the house, Sandra would "play school" and hold English class for them. She took the role very seriously. She was a very strict teacher and well-respected, even by the older boys in her class. What she didn't know was that all these experiences were maturing her beyond her years and preparing her for the future.

Meanwhile, Maria Teresa was also facing the typical challenges all immigrants face as they adjust to their new homeland. Maria Teresa had come from a town with a one-room schoolhouse for all grades. She was advanced, so she had completed school when she was only 10. Now Cata told her she would have to start going to school again. Initially, Maria Teresa balked, but Cata convinced her to "just try it", and she agreed. It was hard for Maria Teresa to go from being at the top of the class in Mexico to struggling in English-speaking classes and receiving "D's" in the U.S. However, even though Sandra was younger, she was always there to assist Maria Teresa with her homework. Maria Teresa worked hard. A year and a half later, she had conquered English, was doing well in regular classes and decided school wasn't so bad after all. Now she did not have to be told. She had learned to love and understand the power of education.

In high school, Maria Teresa was an honor roll student. She took business classes like typing, business, accounting, management electives and even received the "Career Cooperative Award", a recognition given by the teachers to an exemplary student in the business department. Two years later, when Sandra was in high school, she too enrolled in many of the same business classes and even received the same award.

TRUE SISTERS, FUTURE PLANS

When Maria Teresa was 12 years old, she overheard Jose and Cata saying they were planning on adopting her. Her reaction surprised herself. She started crying. Being adopted meant she had to face the reality that her life in Mexico was forever behind her. Also, the thought of being an "adopted child" made her feel abnormal, like she didn't have a "real" family, even though logically, she knew she did. In hindsight, Maria Teresa feels she may have been grieving for the life she left so quickly and easily when she was 11.

Both of us, Sandra and Maria Teresa, have a very positive attitude on life. We believe positive things can come from painful experiences. In Maria Teresa's case, an adoption would mean a streamlined path to legal citizenship. Maria Teresa was adopted, and we rejoiced at being "true" sisters at last.

Maria Teresa had aspirations for college but she also knew she had to pay for it herself. When she was 15, she got a job at McDonald's to help contribute to the household. She didn't have a car, so she often had a 20-minute walk to work. After graduation, she decided to study business at DeVry University and got a good job in her senior year working as an accountant at Superior Coffee, a subsidiary of the Sara Lee Corporation.

Meanwhile, Sandra was also feeling pressure to make a decision about her life's goal. Although her parents always believed in her, she also knew they wouldn't be able to afford college tuition, and they didn't have the experience needed to guide her through the process. She went to see her high school guidance counselor, but he was no help. She made plans to enroll in DeVry. She was conscious that education was her ticket to the American dream.

Sandra always believed that things happen for a reason.

One day her Uncle Jim invited her to his company's "Take Your Child to Work Day". He was a computer programmer at Allstate Insurance and Sandra looked up to him because he was the only family member in a professional position. He also spoke passionately about his job, which she found intriguing. For Sandra, the experience was unforgettable. She thought, "I can't wait to grow up and work here!" To this day, Sandra is grateful to Jim who motivated her, believed in her, and taught her by example that a simple act can truly make a positive difference in someone's life.

A WORKING FAMILY

Everyone in our family was noticing that the Hispanic community was on the rise. Jose had been doing community work at a church ministry named La Red De Protección and could see how immigrants needed direction and help adapting to their new world in the U.S. There were also not many businesses in the suburbs of Chicago that catered to the growing needs of the Hispanic community. He thought about the immigrants who had to take off work and go to "La Villita", a predominantly Mexican neighborhood, in order to complete their tax forms. He wanted to provide good tax and accounting services and training to immigrants, to empower them as they assimilated to the country. He wasn't an accountant himself, but it was 1999 and Maria Teresa had obtained her accounting degree, so Ramos Tax & Services was born. At first, there was no office. We worked from home, preparing tax returns for family members and friends.

Sandra was in college studying computer science and business, so she joined the company part-time. As our company grew by reputation, we opened up our Streamwood office in 2001.

We expanded our services to help customers with their accounting, payroll, auto insurance, vehicle titles and registration, translations, notary public and immigration forms. Now we've added offices in Elgin and Wisconsin.

Today, we are both still traveling through life together in the country that changed our lives. We were each other's maids of honor at our weddings and we live close enough for our children (nine between the two of us!) to have plenty of playtime with their cousins. It's wonderful to work together and see each other often. Through life's ups and downs, we are together to offer support, encouragement and a reminder that opportunity always awaits. For us, our journeys to America made us more than Americans…it made us sisters!

REFLECTION

1. Have you ever had a negative experience result in something positive?

2. Maria Teresa's actual dream about coming to America really happened. Have you ever had an actual "dream" come true? What happened?

3. How has your family's influence empowered you?

BIOGRAPHY

Maria Teresa Ramos and Sandra L. Ramos-Magnani are adoptive sisters and co-founders of Ramos Tax & Services. The company offers individuals and small businesses a variety of professional services including income tax preparation, accounting, payroll, automobile titles, registration and insurance, immigration forms and more.

Currently, Maria Teresa serves as President and heads the small business accounting/payroll sector of the business and the Ramos Income Tax School, which provides training to new tax preparers. Sandra is Vice President and heads insurance and the other affiliate businesses offered through the agency, such as Ramos Insurance, Ramos Financial and Ramos Property Management LLC. The ladies have helped grow the company into three locations (Streamwood and Elgin, Illinois as well as Madison, Wisconsin) with more than 60 employees serving thousands of customers.

For three consecutive years, Maria Teresa and Sandra have been honored with the "Reflecting Excellence Award" from Reflejos, the largest bilingual Latino publication in the northwest Chicago suburbs. They both attended DeVry University. Maria Teresa received her B.S. in accounting and is a licensed Insurance Producer in property and casualty while Sandra holds a B.S. in Computer Information Systems with a minor in accounting. Both sisters are happily married with children who get to see each other often.

Maria Teresa Ramos
MariaTeresa@ramostax.com
(630) 504-0071

Sandra L. Ramos-Magnani
Sandy@ramostax.com
(630) 504-0071

Vivian Martinez-Stachura

"Always be you."

Have you had someone tell you, "You can't go to college, you are not smart enough." "You can't do that job" or "I don't know if you will get that job because you are Latina?" I want to show you that yes you can, and yes you will, even if people tell you otherwise. I am who I am, blessed and successful, not because it was given to me, but because my personal experiences have inspired me to be the Latina woman I am today.

PLANT NOW, HARVEST LATER

Being born and raised on the east side of Aurora, Illinois, I have nothing but great memories. I was raised in a Catholic, hardworking, blue-collar Puerto Rican family where my parents stressed love and always put my brother Tony and me first. We could have had the big house, the nice car, the family vacation, but we didn't because Mom and Dad's priorities were to invest in our education so we would have choices in the future.

I attended Sacred Heart School in Aurora from kindergarten through fourth grade along with my cousins and many family friends. Sacred Heart was an all-Latino school and I felt like I belonged. Then one day our principal announced that Sacred Heart was closing. I worried I would not be with my friends, who were mostly going to go to Archbishop Romero, which was the merging school with Sacred Heart. My cousins were going to St. Joseph's in Aurora. When I asked my parents, they held their heads down and said, "Vivian, you will be going to Our Lady of Good Counsel."

The news totally crushed me. I felt so lost, so scared. I wouldn't have my friends or cousins with me and I would be in a school with no diversity. I thought, "I am not Caucasian and have never been around kids that were different from me. How are they going to accept me?"

When I was 10 and about to start at Good Counsel, my mother sat me down for a talk. She said, "Vivian, I know this is hard, and your first days are going to be difficult. A lot of these kids will be different than you, but you always remember to always be you. Never let anyone make you feel that they are better than you. Kids can be mean, but be strong, and never let them see you cry. You be strong and have God in your heart."

Mom was right. It was tough because I was different. I endured name-calling and bullying. They called me "Fro" because I had short, poofy hair.

How did I overcome the bullying during my grade school years? I remembered the words of advice from my mom. I never let them see me hurt or even cry. I held back my feelings. I just ignored it and tried to be tough and turn it around. I laughed along with the jokes to show it didn't bother me or hurt me.

I kept my chin up, and soon I became one of the strongest, toughest girls in my class. The more I pushed through, the more my confidence shined. I didn't have to change me, I already was me. Once my peers got to know me, I was one of the most popular girls in my class.

NO ONE IS BETTER THAN YOU

After Good Counsel, I attended Rosary High School. There, I felt different because I came from a working class family and lived on the east side of Aurora. Other girls lived in affluent neighborhoods. I rarely had friends over because my friends' parents wouldn't let their daughters come to my "bad neighborhood".

This bothered me. I would talk to my parents about my struggle of being different. The majority of my friends were going to college to become doctors, nurses, lawyers and teachers. I didn't have that in common with them. Their parents were career people. I asked my parents, "What do I have in common with them?"

My parents said they understood it's hard to be around my classmates and their families, knowing they are financially better off than us. "Vivian, no one is better than you and one day those families will see who Vivian Martinez is," they said.

I didn't have a mentality of defeat at Rosary. I actually loved attending there. I made sure I was the best at everything I did. I proved to myself and others that I was not any different. I started to shine. I was involved in many clubs and the school musicals. I danced and sang in the talent shows and my teachers could not believe their eyes. I became captain of the Rosary Dance Team. I was elected Karios Retreat Leader twice- an honor for an underclassman. I overcame my struggles by not playing the victim, but recognizing that some classmates were inferior to me. Then I had to change that mindset and tell myself, I am humble, I come from a humble family upbringing, and my parents sacrificed so much for me to be here because I belong here. I am good enough and smart enough and my future is to graduate and go to college. They believed in me and furthermore, I believed in myself.

I became the first in my family to graduate from college at Aurora University. It was an accomplishment that started a trend for the next family generation. I worked as a fitness instructor for Gold's Gym in Aurora as I struggled to find a full-time job in a failing economy. I prayed for a big opportunity and it came one day when the boss at Gold's asked if I wanted to manage an all-women workout facility. I will never forget what he said. "This is a big opportunity, and it is on you Vivian. You are either going to mess it up and fail completely or you are going to succeed. It's your choice."

I chose to succeed, not fail.

I knew my boss believed in me. He saw my determination throughout the years that I worked with him. I succeeded and treated the women's gym like it was my own business. I set up seminars and spoke about health and fitness. It was an amazing journey, until another opportunity came my way.

OPPORTUNITY KNOCKS

I received an opportunity to work for a major multi-million dollar privately held company which was very different from Gold's and offered advancement. I worked in sales for six months and then was promoted to Assistant Director of Operations. It was one of the most challenging jobs of my life. My V.P. warned me that he wasn't the easiest boss to work for, nor was the president of the company. Right from the beginning, I wasn't accepted. They had bets about when I was going to quit. I was clearly not the candidate they wanted, mainly because I was female.

I understood I was working for a "brutal" boss. Sometimes I was given such unjust problems to solve that I felt like I was in the movie, "The Devil Wears Prada". I was verbally abused daily, in a hostile environment where that was the norm. Every day, my boss tried to make someone cry. I had moments at my desk when I wanted to quit because it was unbearable, but I didn't. Last minute client requests and special demands always seemed to come down on me and my boss. At the end of the day, I was the person that handled the problems.

I was losing myself. The leader I was, the positivity and confidence I once had were slowly fading because of the verbal and mental abuse. I wasn't cheerful and I felt defeated. I knew in my heart this wasn't my personality. I would come home exhausted, mentally drained, depressed, and angry. I would have moments of self-doubt and ask myself, "Is this why I worked so hard in school? Were all my leadership awards a lie? Is this what corporate business is like in the real world?"

THE EYE-OPENING MOMENT

I would think back to my childhood talks with my parents about God and faith where I was told to always have God in my heart. I tried to remember that I was given the necessary tools to help me with my life struggles, and it was my responsibility to take control of them.

One day, I had enough of the job. I told my boss I was going to Wal-Mart, drove into an empty parking lot, sat in silence for a few moments and then had an eye-opening moment. I told myself I had two choices: quit or not give up and persevere, so I could learn more, and take it with me when the next opportunity arose.

I chose option number two. It wasn't in my blood to quit. I thought about my parents and how my father worked and slaved at his job in a factory to give me education and allow me to be part of a big company. I also wasn't going to give anyone the satisfaction of defeating me. I prayed for the strength for the long journey. I told myself, I will gain passion in my job, I will gain respect from my managers and I can "make it happen". In the end, I told myself that I don't work for The Man, I work for the most high. In the Lord I believe and in myself I believe.

Ten years later, I am still in my same position, working in the same department. After years of perseverance, and that eye-opening moment in my car, I gained my sense of self back. I stood my ground and defended myself, even when there was a risk of losing my job. I have proved to others that I don't play around.

The challenges strengthen me as a person. When I feel weak, I pick myself up and start again, and because of that, I gained a lot of respect from my boss. To this day he is still tough, but we have an amazing working relationship. I understand now that he definitely had an "old school" way of leading his employees, but it came from a good place, even though it didn't always feel like it. He always believed in me, and I have learned to read between the lines with him. He recruited me because he saw my passion. He was preparing me for the tough world we live in. He was my mentor when I thought he was my enemy. After ten years, I finally heard the words come out of his mouth, "You passed the test my Vivian; you passed boot camp and graduated to a corporate marine. I am proud of you."

Life is wonderful. Being a Latina in this world is amazing and something to be proud of. We have so many Latinas that have stood up for themselves that they are now sharing their stories and inspiring others. The truth is, there will be bumps in the road, but that is how we learn. I love this quote by Jim Robin's when he talks about life obstacles, "Learning is the beginning of wealth, learning is the beginning of health, learning is the beginning of spirituality, searching and learning is when the miracle process of all begins."

Always remember to be you and don't change for anyone. I am who I am, successful not because it was given to me, but through my experiences. What about you?

REFLECTION

1. If there is one thing about you that you would want change what is it? And why?

2. If your supervisor asked you to do something you didn't feel was right would you do it?

3. Do you have a dream? Would you persevere through the obstacles to achieve it?

4. What beliefs do you carry that you feel is holding you back?

BIOGRAPHY

Vivian is the Director of Operations at Aspen Marketing in West Chicago, Illinois. She has more than 10 years of experience in business, sales marketing, project management, event planning and logistics. She started with Aspen as a representative working for the automotive sector and currently takes on the role of event planning logistics for onsite and offsite events and conferences for the corporate office.

Prior to joining Aspen, Vivian worked in the fitness industry for eight years as a personal trainer and fitness instructor for Bally Total Fitness in Naperville, and Gold's Gym in Aurora Illinois. After Gold's was acquired by Provena Mercy Center, she opened Provena's first women's fitness facility.

Vivian holds a B.S. in Business Administration from Aurora University and an A.A. in Business Science from Wabaonsee Committee College. She is also an AFAA Certificated Personal Trainer and Group Fitness instructor and is a certified dance team coach.

In her free time, Vivian enjoys working out and teaches group fitness classes. She resides in Plainfield, Illinois with her husband and 2-year-old son.

Vivian Martinez
VStachura79@gmail.com
(630) 854-6318

THE MEANING OF LOVE

Raisa Jimenez

"Positive thoughts bring positive outcomes."

In 1997, while visiting my sister in Santo Domingo, Dominican Republic, I assisted at a party where I met one of her neighbors, a young man who became my husband. He was a hard worker from a good family, and a perfect husband for any woman. By then, I was the owner of my own modeling school in Queens, New York. We started to get to know each other and shortly afterwards, I became his wife.

Like everything at the beginning, it was all happiness and fun. We made sure to share every possible moment together. The fun seemed never-ending. Soon after our wedding, I became pregnant with my first baby girl, Raydeli. We decided to make a better life for our family in America, where I had lived since I was 13. For my husband, it was an abrupt change since his parents, siblings, friends, and his dream job were all in the Dominican Republic. Nevertheless, he decided to walk down this unknown path with me.

Once in New York, things started to change. Without realizing it, our hectic lives started to grow in different directions.

The responsibility of taking care of a family at such a young age started to overwhelm me to the point that I stopped taking care of myself. Meanwhile, the tender, sympathetic, sweet ideal man that I married gradually disappeared, and even turned into a complete stranger. Alcohol became his best friend, and verbal, psychological, and physical abuse became common. I began to have more fear for him than respect. By then, I had already given birth to my second child, Jose.

TIME OF CONFUSION

One summer night, we had a family party at our house that lasted past midnight. We had been celebrating the birthday of one of my brother-in-laws all day. The alcohol had started to take effect on my husband. His arrogance and self-centeredness took control. There were a few guests still left in the house and he kicked them out for no reason at all. He became aggressive and the neighbors heard his screams from a couple houses down.

Once we were alone, I put the kids to bed. Raydeli was nine years old, Jose was eight and Julia was four. I can still remember seeing the fear in their eyes and how my Jose came running to me, trying to protect me from his father's attack. The kids yelled and cried at the same time for him to let me go and get out of the room, but he continued to ignore them. Finally, he decided to leave, but not before he made it clear that I wasn't a woman to him, he didn't love me, and that women who were better than me were available around every corner.

I wanted to take my kids and run far away... but where?

Who could I have explained my situation to without creating more problems? Who could I draw upon? I was embarrassed to tell my family what was happening with him for so many years. How could I tell them the humiliation that I had gone through while they were thinking that our marriage was "perfect"? I did not sleep that night. Instead I spent the night asking, why me? What did I do wrong to deserve this?

The following morning, like every morning, I got the kids ready and took them to school before going to work. The day was hard and went by slowly. I needed to speak to someone. I needed to vent and let everything out. Without even noticing, I drove straight to my sister's house right after work. It seemed like she knew I needed her and would find my way to her. When she saw me, she hugged me tightly and invited me in. I broke down, cried, and tried to express everything I was feeling. We spent hours talking.

LOSING FEAR

That day I started to understand why I needed to make changes, even though it would be hard. I had to accept the fact that I was going through abuse by the person closest to me.... MY HUSBAND!! It was time to stop housing all my pain and suffering. I understood that it was time to ask for help from my family.

I am a strong believer in the law of attraction. If you think you are going to fall down and don't have a positive outlook about it, you will. In that moment, I fell, yet I wasn't ready to stay down.

I was ready to continue with my life, with new perspectives, and new projects. I believe that positive thoughts bring positive outcomes.

Many of us know that we have to make a decision, but due to fear and cowardice, we postpone it, thinking that by delaying it, it will magically disappear. Unfortunately, it's not like that. For me, it wasn't easy to stay calm and positive. It was a long and difficult process, but I was determined to change the situation. So I focused on bringing positive things into my life; all those things that help me become a happier and better human being. I had the opportunity to help my husband overcome his alcoholism and gain control of his life again.

Maybe we should reevaluate our decisions after we lose enthusiasm and excitement. Many times, we attach ourselves to people and things without letting the cycle of life flow, or allowing better opportunities into our lives.

Today I feel blessed to have marvelous people by my side. In one way or another, they stick around and are there to help me when I need them. In the same way, I'm there for them if they ever need me.

Today I understand that humiliating and abusing someone is not love. Love is respecting, valuing, and caring for another. In order to feel love for someone, you need to feel it for yourself first. You need to love and value yourself for who you are. I am open to this new chapter of life and blessing all the good it brings!

REFLECTION

1. How do you realize that the time has come to make a life-changing decision?
2. How much time do you spend thinking about what others think and say about you?
3. What things do you do daily that help you value yourself?

BIOGRAPHY

Raisa was born in the Dominican Republic, the youngest of five children. She was raised by her siblings, as her mother had already immigrated to the U.S. As a child, she was always interested in beauty and decided to study modeling in New York City. At the age of 17, Raisa was inspired to open her own modeling school in the borough of Queens, New York. She educated young girls between the ages of 5 and 18 in the art of modeling, personal development, presence, and protocol. She owned a beauty salon for approximately two years with her sister and is currently working towards opening an Aesthetic Spa Center in Queens. She is the proud mother of three children, Raydeli (17), Jose (16), and Julia (12).

Raisa Jimenez
rjs.success23@gmail.com
(646) 703-6260

Fabiola Haro

"Whatever you do, do it with passion. The rest comes by itself."

I was born on February 20, 1978 in Cuajimalpa, D.F., Mexico. Raised in a family with three brothers and four sisters, we lived an economically stable life. For the first seven years of my childhood, I lived in a neighborhood that my father owned. He had a large amount of land with houses that he rented out.

My father was a hard-working man that always did well in his business ventures, but he had two vices: drinking and cockfighting. My mother was a submissive woman, raising eight children by herself including her son Luis who at a very young age fell from the rooftop. He suffered serious brain injuries. This event was a big tragedy for the family, but it impacted my mother the most. My father, consumed with his vices, left my mother to deal with her children on her own. I slept in a small house with my grandmother. One day, as I was helping her sew, my older sister Imelda came and told my grandmother that our mother had abandoned us.

I remembered it like it was a nightmare. I was five years old and I kept myself occupied between school, my grandma's house, and sleep because I didn't want to think, hear, or even ask why my mother had abandoned all her children. Surely it was my father's fault she left. This event impacted me greatly. After a year, my mother returned and it felt like a dream. Shortly afterwards, my grandmother passed away and it felt like she had abandoned me too. I had lost the person I slept with, prayed with, and someone I loved dearly.

After my grandmother's death, my father sold his "neighborhood" and we migrated to another state in Mexico called Aguascalientes to the marvelous town of Malpaso. It was filled with rivers and a dam, a town square and a wonderful church. It was like waking up from a nightmare and living a dream. I grew up in Malpaso. It was where I went to school, learned to swim, and where I felt most free.

I graduated from la secundaria, which is the equivalent of middle school, and started la preparatoria, which prepares you for university. I felt proud of myself because none of my five older siblings had graduated from la secundaria, much less gone on to la preparatoria, and I was the first to continue with my studies. When I was 12 years old, three of my older siblings migrated to the U.S. to fend for themselves and make their fortune. They no longer wanted to depend on my father. He was a man who always gave us everything but never taught us how to be independent; he liked to have his children be dependent on him so he felt in control.

Shortly after turning 15, I received a call from my sister Imelda in America. She wanted to bring me to the U.S. to study and work, a dream of mine that I had not yet thought about. My father would not let me come to the U.S. because he said I had everything already: a house, school, and food.

After much convincing from my sister, I was allowed to go. My siblings took care of all the arrangements and in August 1993, I traveled to the U.S. After days on the border, I was finally able to cross and went to Los Angeles, California. From there I traveled to Chicago, Illinois and reunited with my siblings. After a month, Imelda told me I could not go to school because she could not get the permits, but I was going to work in the cleaning company she worked for.

A NEW WORLD

I woke up from my dream of learning English and I began working in this new world where everything was different. I had to learn new things and meet new people, and in meeting these new people, I met the love of my life, Marco. He was the supervisor of the company where I began to work. I was 17 and he was 21 when we fell in love and after eight months of dating, I became pregnant. My brothers and sister didn't know I was pregnant until they decided that we had to go back to Mexico.

Knowing this, Marco tried to talk to my siblings but they didn't accept him and told me I needed to get an abortion and return to Mexico. After hearing this, Marco asked me to live with him because he loved his child and wasn't going to permit something like that. My new world began to change. My brothers were angry with me and stopped speaking to me. They returned to Mexico.

Marco and I moved to Miami, Florida to live with his family, his mom, and his sister. Marco worked as an electrician with his uncle and I stayed at home. After nine months, my daughter Cristina was born. I was 18, illegal, and didn't know how to speak English so the only thing I could do was stay at home taking care of my daughter and the house. After Cristina turned three, I decided that I needed to get a job in order to contribute and get ahead. The easiest work for an illegal who doesn't speak English is cleaning houses.

I worked cleaning houses for a long time and it was a little extra money. When Cristina was six years old, Marco and I decided to have another child. After our second daughter was born, we got approved for a loan on a house. What joy it was to have our own little home.

THE AMERICAN DREAM

Our home would be the first American dream. The following year, Marco's residency got approved. What joy, another dream was accomplished! After a few months of Marco being a resident, he decided to travel to Guatemala, his home country, to visit his grandfather who he hadn't seen in 18 years. On this trip, Marco met a woman he seemed to fall in love with. He came back to Miami a different man. Months passed and he wanted a divorce. He abandoned me and the children to be with that woman.

Seeing my dreams fall apart little by little, I couldn't stay illegal without speaking English. I began learning basic English and learning to become an assistant accountant while I continued cleaning houses. I couldn't divorce Marco until I became a resident. I couldn't leave my daughters if I was deported back to Mexico. My mother abandoned her children for some reason, but I would not abandon my daughters for any reason. I had to keep holding on to the American Dream.

THE REAL AMERICAN DREAM

Marco going to Guatemala had to happen in order for me to make the decision to study and fight for my residency in the United States. I was suffering a lot and I could not understand why all this was happening to me. I could not imagine being deported and leaving my daughters behind. In between melancholy and internal depression, I started to get white spots on my skin, vitiligo. But all this didn't matter to me. I had to keep on going and continue fighting. I began filling out the immigration papers and shortly afterwards, I was detained by I.C.E. (Immigration and Customs Enforcement) who put me under house arrest for six months. Marco was in his other life, without caring what happened to his daughters. But I am eternally grateful for the support of my mother and sister-in-law who helped me through all this.

Finally, after eleven months, my lawyer called me to go in front of the immigration court. While in court, my residency was approved. I could not believe it. Everything truly does happen for a reason.

With a legal status and knowing a little English, I began

working at a restaurant as a cashier with a desire to learn everything. After five months of working for that restaurant and learning how to manage the store, I was promoted to assistant manager. I was truly living the real American dream. I had legal papers, a basic knowledge of English, a house to fight for, a driver's license, a legal job, and my daughters who were the most important thing to me....yet I wanted more.

I continued to study and got classes in order to prepare taxes. Later, I had the opportunity to prepare taxes for the IRS for two years as a volunteer. I couldn't believe that I was achieving all this. After working for a year with this restaurant, a pizza chain with more than eight stores, the owner of one of these stores, Mr. Atienza approached me and asked me to work for him. Without a second thought, I accepted his proposal. In less than a year I had become a general manager. I didn't know the responsibilities of a general manager but I accepted anyway because I knew I could learn and do well.

After nine months of working for Mr. Atienza, who trusted me blindly, I was moved to one of his biggest stores. I was doing an exceptional job and I had to keep on learning. Without realizing it, I became the only female general manager in the company. I was very happy and grateful to Mr. Atienza, who believed in me. Then, because of personal problems, Mr. Atienza returned his stores to Mr. Prats, the CEO of the company. While working for Mr. Prats, I was moved to another store which was the headquarters, and the largest store in the corporation.

Months passed and Marco separated from the woman he

met in Guatemala. She lived in Guatemala while he lived here in the U.S. I don't know what type of relationship that was, but Marco wanted to return to his family. Marco and I got back together and our daughters are happy to have their dad at home. I couldn't believe that everything happened for a reason.

At the headquarters, I had to learn many new things as general manager such as payroll, inventory, labor, and food costs just to name a few, but as if that were not enough, I also had to train assistant managers, general managers, and new store owners. How could I have accomplished all of this without going to school for this or anyone training me? It was the passion and desire to learn.

However, all of these responsibilities were keeping me from my daughters, who needed me at home. I was always working and neglecting the time I had with them. I decided to leave the restaurant and gave my notice to Mr. Prats. Two months after I quit, Mr. Prats contacted me to tell me that he was recommending me for a Cuban restaurant chain that had more than five stores and 700 employees. I thought it was a great idea to be able to learn how another restaurant worked. I began working as an assistant manager for the company in September 2013. Everything was different: the food, employees, system of working, etc. but I wanted to learn it all. In May 2015, they offered me the position of General Manager. I gladly accepted and in June, I officially became the first female General Manager in the company, hoping that in the near future I can open a restaurant of my own.

REFLECTION

1. What do you do when it feels like everyone has abandoned you?

2. What comes first, your job or your family? Or can there be a balance between them?

3. What is your dream? What can you do to accomplish it?

BIOGRAPHY

Fabiola Haro is the General Manager of Sergio's Restaurant, a Cuban kitchen and bar in Miami. Originally from Mexico, Fabiola came to the U.S. illegally at the age of 16, not knowing how to speak English, but yearning for the American dream. After only six years in the restaurant industry, and starting at the bottom, she worked her way up to become the first female general manager at Sergio's.

Throughout her career in the restaurant industry, she has experienced the many different aspects of managing a restaurant on a daily basis and has learned about operations, budgeting, personnel, and more. She also has volunteered and prepared taxes for the IRS. Fabiola lives by the saying: "whatever you do, do it with passion," and her passion is in the restaurant industry. She loves seeing a customer leave happy and one of her lifelong goals is to own her own restaurant.

Fabiola has been married for 20 years to her husband, Marco Gomez, and has two daughters, Cristina (19) and Ashley (12). Family is very important to her and she loves spending time with her loved ones.

Fabiola Haro
harofabiola@gmail.com
(786) 312-8997

Lourdes Martinez

"Grow organically and give opportunity to other people."

I am a true Mexican-American. I was born in California, but raised in Mexico because my parents decided to go back to their hometown a few months after I was born. I remember when I was seven years old, my uncle Pablito came to Mexico and talked to my parents. He told them they should let me go back to the U.S. so I could learn English, since I was a U.S. citizen. My mom talked to me about it and I liked the idea. Being away from my brother and having a different family for a year sounded like a good deal at that age.

AN AMERICAN IN MEXICO

I went back and forth for four years and then my family started to grow. Two more brothers, Pedro and David, were added to the family. Now it was hard for me to leave because I had two little brothers to love and take care of. I decided to stay, attend school in Mexico and help my dad with his business. He had two grocery stores and I had to help him there after school.

Being raised in Mexico as a U.S. citizen became a little

harder for me because, believe it or not, there is racism in Mexico. When my schoolmates found out I was born in another country, they would call me names such as Bolilla, Chicana, Gringa, and Pocha. I did not like them at all; they made me feel I was different. Also, I was not good at making friends and the few friends I had lived very far from me. After school, I decided to just stay focused on my dad's business.

When I was 14 years old, I heard that the family business was not going well and that my dad and I had to move to Chicago. To top it off, my parent's relationship was not working out anymore and they decided to separate. I came to live with my dad, but because he didn't have an apartment, he told me to stay with my aunt Lety. She was very nice to me, but since she worked the second shift, her sister-in-law took care of my cousins and me. She always saw them as angels and me as the rebel kid.

After a while, I started to have problems. One day, my aunt talked to my dad and told him that as much as she loved me, she was not able to pay as much attention to me as I needed. She said the best solution would be to look for another place for me to live. At that time, my dad was not able to afford an apartment for both of us, even though I offered to work after school. He had many debts in Mexico, which is how he spent his paycheck.

At the age of 16, I went to live with his cousin, who was a single mother and had a girl the same age as me. I thought this was going to be fun. I got a job in a small restaurant after school and made my own money, helped with rent and bought my own things. But once I started to make money, jealousy came with it. One day my dad's cousin told me I focused too much on making money and that eventually I would forget about school and concentrate only on working, while her daughter would have a career and be a successful woman. Three months later, her daughter became pregnant and the rest is history.

After a lot of hard work, my dad was able to afford an apartment, so I went to Mexico to bring my older brother to live with us. Since we were raised by our father through our teenage years, people always said that eventually I would become pregnant and that my brother and I would become drug addicts, etc. But my dad always talked to us and told us to prove everybody wrong.

I remember that since my dad would send money to Mexico for my younger brothers, we couldn't afford a fridge. During the winter, we had to put our food by the entrance for it to stay cold. One of my dad's cousins came to visit very often and I would fight with him because he would step on our ham unintentionally. However, even though we didn't have much, we were very happy.

FALSE STARTS

When I graduated from high school, I learned about the insurance industry and talked to my dad about it. He offered to pay for my insurance license because he liked the idea of me jumping into an industry with a good future. But at that age, I didn't appreciate the opportunity and I let my license lapse.

I decided to go to Mexico to see my mom and my younger brothers. When I was there, I decided to stay with my mom and go to school to be a psychologist. All was going as planned, but six months later, my mom and I got into an argument and I decided to try to live on my own. It was then I realized how hard it is for undocumented people to live in the U.S. because I went through the same thing in Mexico. I could not get a decent job to pay my bills. A friend I met in Mexico told me of a modeling agency where they didn't ask for papers to work, so I decided to do that for a while. I made enough to pay my bills and put food on the table, but coming back to an empty place every day made me realize how good I had had it with my dad and brother.

I lived like this for a while and then decided to call my dad to ask if I could go back home. Deciding to go back to the U.S. made me realize I had to be independent and whatever decision I made would affect only me. When I called, I found out he had gotten married and things had changed in the house. So because of my stubbornness, I decided to go to Kansas with one of my aunts.

With her, I didn't think there would be any problems because she was my mom's oldest sister and my uncle was my dad's oldest brother, so they were family on both ends. Their oldest daughter, Melin, was like a sister to me more than a cousin. I started to work in a car insurance agency and made good money. I helped with rent and also took my two cousins to the mall to buy clothes. Everything was going well until I noticed there was machismo in the house. My oldest cousins were very demanding with the girl cousins and since I was a bit of a tomboy, I never let anybody boss me around. I fought my battle until I was thrown out the door, back to Chicago.

LIFE AND CHANGE

I was glad I was home and now I had to get serious about my life and goals. I was 20 years old and I had to make a decision. I talked to my dad about going back into the insurance industry, but this time he told me I had to earn it myself. One of my friends told me his dad was hiring somebody to clean bathrooms in a hotel at night and I accepted, thinking it was going to be a temporary position. But every time I had the money to take the insurance test, I would fall asleep during the test. After staying at the position for a while, a friend I made at the hotel got me a better job in the hotel's gift shop. Since I worked in the morning, I passed the test without sleeping and moved on with my plans.

After a while, I met a guy who was very supportive of my crazy dreams and got married. My husband, Baudelio Martinez, made me feel I finally had a place I could call my own and nobody could push me away from it. We had two wonderful kids, Arely and Junior, who inspired me to keep on following my dreams of been independent and making a good living in the insurance industry.

My mother-in-law was a very important piece of my success. While I was able to pursue my dreams, she became the pillar of my house and a second mom to me. Because of my children, the relationship between my mom and I got better and she became more involved in my life.

After trying my luck with different companies and finding out about a better one every day, I came across a woman who told me her husband needed a Hispanic translator to enroll for voluntary benefits at his company. I asked the insurance company if I could subcontract with them since I had my insurance license. They said yes! In two days, I made more money than I could have done in two months in any other job or company, and that is when I realized I was home. Colonial Life has been a good company for me.

One time, somebody told me that because of my background, it is easy for me to quit and move forward. But I realized I don't quit — I change. When you believe and love what you do, you don't quit on what you believe. You quit on the people who don't have the same vision, and that is what I did. By being part of Colonial Life, I have been able to help a lot of families avoid bankruptcy when they experienced unexpected life changes. This is something that makes me feel proud of what I do.

I was able to qualify for a trip to Alaska with the company and I talked to Tim McGill, the vice president of sales in our region, about being a district manager. He believed in me and told me to go for it. I've been putting my heart into this business and he knew that I would become a good manager.

Robert Horton, the trainer of one of Colonial Life's sales classes at the time, talked to me about being a business owner and opening my own agency. I called it AGSANT Group Inc. Being an entrepreneur makes me put skin in the game and run the show better. I remember one of my predecessors saying that in this business you've got to let the big dog eat first, but that is something I don't believe in. I believe you need to grow organically from the bottom up, and to give opportunity to other people to make money and fall in love with what they do in this industry. If you help your people make money, they will become your best ally and you can count on them to grow your business in a stronger way. This is better trying to work on your own and do everything by yourself.

My territory manager Michael Smith and I have the same beliefs. He had a vision for me and encouraged me to take a leadership role in Colonial Life's Hispanic initiative. I've been very involved in it and have even became the face of the company on some of their recruiting materials.

Thanks to my manager's support, I've been able to grow in the Hispanic industry, and Colonial Life has been the key to my success. I was able to join different organizations like Hispanic Pro, the Illinois Hispanic Chamber of Commerce, and the Aurora Regional Chamber of Commerce. I've been able to get involved in the community and be known for what I do in my business.

I live by a quote that I heard once:

"Your future is unlimited, the world is your territory, mankind is your business and God is your boss."

REFLECTION

1. When something is not going your way, do you quit or change?

2. What changes can you make to enhance your life?

3. Are you at home in any country other than where you live?

BIOGRAPHY

Lourdes Martinez has been in the insurance industry for 17 years. She is the founder of Agsant Group Inc. since 2009 and represents Colonial Life, which is a company that works directly with businesses to help with the attraction and retention of key employees as well as help them navigate through the obstacles they face with the new laws and regulations of the health care reform.

Because of the ten years of experience with Colonial Life, she was chosen to represent the Hispanic industry in the Midwest region. At Colonial Life she has been awarded the Achieving Continuous Excellence Award, Leaders Conference Qualifier as well as Silver Premium Pacesetter Award. She enjoys being a part of the community and to spend quality time with her family and friends.

Lourdes Martinez
Lourdes.Martinez@coloniallife.com
(708) 299-5859

"BEING" NOT JUST "DOING"

Sandra X. Pradas Martin

*"Our life and our success will be measured by the quality
of the life we lead and the lives we touch."*

I was on my bedroom floor reviewing my First Communion gifts. There was one that really caught my attention. It was a plaque with my name along with a definition and description for the meaning of "Sandra". I remember sitting on the rug, still in my gown, settling in after a large, fun celebration with family. With my older and younger siblings sprinkled throughout the house, I was alone in my room and reflecting on this one gift. There it was, in black and white: "Sandra - helper of mankind/ defender of man".

I remember that afternoon because this particular gift had a deep and lasting impact that struck me like a "call to action". It resonated with me in a way that felt familiar yet unclear, achievable yet daunting, great yet humbling. I sat there digesting the story of my name. This gift reinforced something I have always known somewhere deep down in a place where my seven-year-old self couldn't quite explain-- I had (and still have) a greater purpose.

It was an awesome feeling of strength and courage because in that moment, I remember embracing "Sandra" and all that I was and still am capable of becoming. You see, I've always thought of my childhood akin to the story of the ugly duckling who turned into a swan.

THE EMERGING SANDRA

In school, amidst all the other influences outside our families, the road to "Sandra" was not a smooth one. I struggled with self-esteem, self-confidence and "owning" my voice. In my early school age days, I was teased and singled out. What was I teased for? Well, the details are not as important as what I later learned as I walked away. It was an important life lesson that stands true for me today: what we remember depends on how something made us feel. Be it good or bad, positive or negative, our memories come from our emotional response to an event, not necessarily the actions or words that were used.

Our childhood is such an impressionable time where so many experiences, relationships, and interactions are shaping our thoughts, attitudes, and perspectives. I remember those days in first and second grade, coming home crying because I felt like I didn't belong. Those were the days I'd be in my room with my sister and she'd sit with me and coach me on what to say, how to respond, and how to find better friends. My sister, who is four years my senior, has always been my advocate. Our sisterhood is a special relationship. Whether it was stuff at school, home, or anything else in between, we practiced the art of "talking things through". In fact, this was a practiced art form that came from my parents who set the stage for conversations and dialogue on a nightly basis around the dinner table. It didn't take long before the teasing and bad attitudes of others in school had me believing I lacked something.

As is common, there's always something in our past that triggers our negative self-talk, and these were the years when my inner critic – that negative voice in my head– really began to take shape. I questioned, "Am I good enough? Smart enough? Pretty enough?" We all have these voices and these were the ones holding me back, popping up in those moments that would stop me from making myself vulnerable – which only served to prevent me from realizing my potential.

Despite this invisible wall I was creating for myself, I knew deep down that that I was more than what others were telling me. And on my First Communion day, my younger self was "at the right place, at the right time" for me to be open and receptive to deeper reflections of "what's my purpose?"

As a mother, I carry this lesson with me everyday. I make a conscious and deliberate effort to be attuned to the memories I'm creating for me and my family. Like all parents, I have my moments when I'm less than proud of how I handled something or feel guilty of what I said. So what do I do? I try to stop myself from going through that unproductive downward spiral of "if only I said..." or "if only I did...".

Instead, I try to get out of my own head and out of my own way. I try to find ways I can identify the opportunity in something. I ask myself, how can I turn this around? What can I do about it? How can I respond differently? What's the opportunity here? What's the message or lesson in this? Then, the power is taking it a step further. I try asking my children similar reflective questions – the kind of questions that will help them process what's going on so they can, more consciously, create their own emotional memory and experience.

FINDING PURPOSE

I no longer believe in coincidences, but rather that things in our life are revealed to us at different times to serve as pointers, directives and lessons. Then, it is our level of awareness that decides how ready we are to connect the dots and understand the deeper meaning of those lessons, events, situations, and circumstances.

Shortly after my Communion, I spent more time thinking about what I would be when I grew up. In third grade, I remember having to write a book report on a career we would like to pursue. I was so influenced by what was happening for me in school that child psychology quickly grabbed my interest. I was eager to learn what I could about psychology. I remember talking to my parents about it with excitement. It was as if I had connected with this thing that was bigger than me, and could help other kids feel better and stronger about themselves. As I got older, I was convinced this was my path and each of my professional experiences have involved some kind of social service and therapeutic work.

Then I also began to tune into another very important message. My maternal grandmother passed away when I was twelve years old. She was an integral part of our family and her loss hit me hard. My mother and "grandma" - that's what we called her because she said abuela sounded too old - were both very close. Her death was a significant event in my life and we mourned her for quite some time.

Shortly after listening to my eldest brother's eulogy of our grandmother, I remember reading the obituaries one Sunday morning, just out of curiosity and empathy for others who were also experiencing a loss. I had my own awakening. Our life and our success will be measured by the quality of the life we lead and the lives we touch. I remember thinking to myself that it won't be my job that stands at the pulpit or writes my farewell, but my family and friends who will join together in remembrance of what I did and how I did it.

In that moment, there was another seed planted. I realized that no matter what I would decide to pursue for a career, what would matter most is how I was, not what I did. From the resistant little girl undergoing AIDS treatment when I volunteered as a teen at Schneider's Children's Hospital, to the bipolar patient who wrote me a very special thank you note upon his discharge at Kings County Psychiatric Hospital during my time as an activity therapist, or the mom who recently wrote a testimonial sharing her gratitude for our work changing her family's dynamics into a more positive, collaborative and loving experience - I've tried to walk my talk to "be" and not just "do."

As I reflect on my journey of purpose and tale of personal transformation, I am at peace with how things have unfolded in my life. I really believe that my family's support, love, and attention were pivotal in offsetting my challenges in school. I have deep values rooted in the power of family. I think they have encouraged me to recognize that we're more powerful when we're in the company of those that see our potential and champion us all along the way.

My parents often chuckle as they tell the story of when I was six or seven years old and had done something "bad" that I felt very guilty about. They can't remember what I did, but they do remember how I wrote out my own punishment and apology. I left it on my father's night table for him to read when he got home from work. To this day, my dad shares with me that he knew I was "sensitive in a different way", that I was emotionally self-aware and that he didn't need to "come down on me" for things. Others have told me that I'm an old soul. Perhaps the latter is true as well, for I have always felt a calling to do and be more in this life and I know I need to honor it.

THE PARENT LEADER

As an adult, married with two children, I'm realizing even more what it means to be "Sandra: helper of mankind/defender of man". Becoming a mother has pushed me even further to reflect on my personal growth because there is no greater mirror in our life than our children. When it comes to parenting in the early formative and developmental years, I have found great truth in the saying "you get what you put in". I've chosen my profession as a parent and leadership coach because it is here where I feel the most alignment between all the spheres that make up my life.

I truly believe professional success is linked to our personal success, and that a fulfilling life comes from empowering the true (most inner) potential of both ourselves and our family. I intimately know and understand the demands that our roles as parents require, and I'm very realistic that we all have "stuff" that we bring to the table. Through my work, my goal has become to empower ourselves as parents while empowering our kids. All too often we question ourselves and ask if we're doing the right thing or if we're doing enough. Then our own internal parenting critic pops up and guilt surfaces and makes its way into our parenting. Every experience in my journey has taught me that to find answers we must go beyond the surface, and it's no different when it comes to parenting.

One of the key ways I'm fulfilling my purpose is by redefining my role as parent to include the role of leader. It's a profound shift to approach my parenting this way. There has been an incredible and positive momentum in the career world to develop inspirational leadership through trainings, workshops, etc. However, I've found leadership to be an even more necessary and intentional skill to apply in our homes. Our families begin to thrive when we start to think, feel and act like the leaders we are meant to be. The question is not whether or not we are leaders, but how well we lead. To parent with leadership means to lead our children and our family to their best potential. It means owning our ability to inspire, motivate, champion, learn, listen, and develop values around wanting to do the right thing.

I'm proud of my journey and to have arrived at a place where I'm trying to live consciously as a mother, wife, daughter, sister and friend. Every day I make a conscious effort to walk my talk for more inspired and empowered living with hopes that my children become the best versions of themselves and make their impact on this world. Whenever my kids hit a rough patch and begin to doubt themselves, I remind them of our family mantra and together we say, "Si puedo, si puedo, si puedo y lo haces."

REFLECTION

1. The best way to teach love is to be love. How are you being love?

2. Anytime we attach a label to something we create a limit. What label are you using and how is it limiting you?

3. How committed are you to making a change?

BIOGRAPHY

Sandra X. Pradas Martin is a born and raised New Yorker and mother of two. As a first generation American, it is a priority to raise her children bi-lingual – honoring the Bolivian, Spanish, Colombian and Cuban roots of her and her husband. Sandra intimately knows what it takes to juggle competing demands and priorities as she navigates the responsibilities of her various roles inside and outside the home.

Sandra is the owner and founder of Self Balanced Solutions, LLC, a coaching and self-improvement company. Merging her worlds of parenting, coaching and previous leadership work, she is on a mission to help parents go from surviving to thriving in their parenting by redefining leadership in the workplace to leadership in the home. "Parenting with Leadership" supports parents with a unique assessment tool, process and system that removes tension, guilt, conflict and stress while improving the positive power and influence of leadership in the home.

Sandra has spent 14 years in social service work, education empowerment and personal development. She is a graduate of Fordham University, Institute for Professional Excellence in Coaching (iPEC), a certified Energy Leadership Master Practitioner (ELI-MP), and a member of the International Coach Federation (ICF) and its local New York City ICF chapter.

Sandra X. Pradas Martin
sandra@selfbalancedsolutions.com
(917) 620-5122)

Jackie Camacho-Ruiz

**ENTREPRENEUR, AUTHOR, SPEAKER, PHILANTHROPIST,
TODAY'S INSPIRED LATINA FOUNDER.**

Jacqueline Camacho-Ruiz is an award-winning entrepreneur, international speaker, philanthropist and author of eight books, including The Little Book of Business Secrets that work published in 2010. She is founder of The Fig Factor Foundation focused on unleashing the amazing in young Latinas. Jacqueline is a regular guest on local and national TV, radio and print publications.

She has received many prestigious awards, including "Influential Women in Business Award," "Entrepreneurial Excellence" Award and "Annual Awards for Business Excellence" by Daily Herald Business Ledger, "Best Under 40" by Suburban Life, "Unsung Hero" by the City of Aurora and "Woman of Distinction" by Kane County Magazine. She currently serves on the board of the Fox Valley Entrepreneurship Center and The Fig Factor Foundation. As a two-time cancer survivor, Jacqueline possesses wisdom about life well beyond her years. She lives in the Midwest with her husband and business partner, Juan Pablo Ruiz, and her two children. In her spare time, Jackie enjoys flying airplanes, racing cars and experiencing the beauty of life.

For more information, visit www.jackiecamacho.com.